AF879573

Sports Law in Bosnia and Herzegovina

Sports Law in Bosnia and Herzegovina

Sabrina Buljubasic

This book was originally published as a monograph in the International Encyclopaedia of Laws/Sports Law.

Founding Editor: Roger Blanpain
General Editor: Frank Hendrickx
Volume Editor: Michele Colucci

Wolters Kluwer

Published by:
Kluwer Law International B.V.
PO Box 316
2400 AH Alphen aan den Rijn
The Netherlands
E-mail: lrs-sales@wolterskluwer.com
Website: www.wolterskluwer.com/en/solutions/kluwerlawinternational

Sold and distributed by:
Wolters Kluwer Legal & Regulatory U.S.
920 Links Avenue
Landisville, PA 17538
United States of America
E-mail: customer.service@wolterskluwer.com

ISBN 978-94-035-4097-9

e-Book: ISBN 978-94-035-4117-4
web-PDF: ISBN 978-94-035-4107-5

Printed in the Netherlands.

The Author

Sabrina Buljubasic is a Football CEO Adviser, Former Professional Football Player, and International Sports Lawyer. Sabrina is recognized as the first-ever woman to be the CEO of FK Sarajevo. While at FK Sarajevo, she has achieved four major trophies, the first-ever double titles and back-to-back league titles in the club's history. Off the pitch, Sabrina designed the signing agreement of the stadium for FK Sarajevo Football Club. Due to her CEO achievements, she was named Leaders 40 under 40 Award. Currently, Sabrina is the Co-Founder of Dynami Sports Group and conducts CEO & Football Management Workshops for Football Clubs.

The Author

Table of Contents

List of Abbreviations

ADA	Anti-doping Control Agency
BiH	Bosnia and Herzegovina
CAS	Court of Arbitration for Sport
FA	Football Association
FBiH	Federation Entity of Bosnia and Herzegovina
FIFA	*Fédération Internationale de Football Association*/French for International Federation of Association Football
IOC	International Olympic Committee
LGE-BiH	Law on Gender Equality in Bosnia and Herzegovina
NS/FS BiH	National Football Association of Bosnia and Herzegovina
OCBiH	Bosnia and Herzegovina Olympic Committee
RS	Republika Srpska Entity of Bosnia and Herzegovina
UEFA	*Union des Associations Européennes de Football*/French for Union of European Football Associations
WADA	World Anti-doping Agency

List of Abbreviations

General Introduction

§1. General Background

1. To consider the aspect of sports law within Bosnia and Herzegovina (BiH), we must consider some of the country's history and forming independency. The background information will allow us to understand the legal system, thus the sports regulations and laws within BiH. The country of BiH was once part of a union, which was known as Yugoslavia, which was formed with six other countries in the region (BiH, Croatia, Serbia, Montenegro, Slovenia, Kosovo, Macedonia, now called North Macedonia). Yugoslavia was a great sporting nation, especially basketball and football. The national teams were recognized around the world, achieving success in football and basketball against other top-ranked national teams in the world. The success of Yugoslavia and the love of sports are still active within the different countries that split from Yugoslavia.

2. To understand the country's background, we must look at the early 1990s when BiH was involved in a civil war (other regional countries were involved), previously in the period between 1992 and 1995 before breaking independent from Yugoslavia. One of the main factors for the war was the independency of the countries and, in this particular circumstance, that of BiH, which sought independence from Yugoslavia, which was in the hands of Serbia and Montenegro at the time. With an in-depth analysis of the country of BiH, it can be concluded that the structure of the country has one of the most complicated systems in the world, which affects each part of the country. When we discuss the system, in this particular context, we are pointing out the government structure and the legal one at most. The system is yet to be considered unified as BiH is a country that is split into two different entities and the Brcko District. The lack of a country being centralized takes a toll on the operational aspect of the country as a whole. The population of BiH stacks up to a small number of 3.5 million, and considering the war that occurred, the population is less because people fled to set up a safe life for their families abroad. It is sure that the country is still developing after the war and that even though it is considered a small country, it truly has a love for sports, which has been carried to each region of the country.

3. In 1995, the Daytona Agreement[1] was signed under the framework that the country would be split with Bosnians, Croatians, and Serbians (Muslim, Catholic,

1. *See* Daytona Framework Agreement (Daytona 1995).

Orthodox), which make up the country that is called BiH. The split of the country led to the certain formation of the split of the two entities within BiH, keeping in mind the following: The *Federation* (mixed but mostly Bosnians/Croats), *Republika Srpska* (most Serbian/Orthodox) and not an entity but a separate jurisdiction—*Brcko District* (mixed/Serbs). The reasoning for the split and the signing of the Dayton was to end the war and find a compromise in which all three ethnic groups would be represented and the separation of jurisdictions with the entities and Brcko District. In the system of the Daytona, the most complicated of the signings of such was the physical split on the map and between the people, which still to this day lies between the different entities.

4. The law system also had to be revised to fulfill the complicated structure of the separation of the jurisdictions. The main factor to be considered from the above paragraph is that an agreement was made to end the war, but this agreement made an enormous impact on the day-to-day life of people living in BiH. If we take into consideration that Yugoslav had a population of more than 20 million people and after the split, BiH was left with a population under 4 million, the development of sports is still on the rise for the small country, as is the country as a whole.

5. The governmental structure is one of the most complicated systems, but to further make the structure difficult is the legal framework that we must mention to understand the full concept with the legal aspects of BiH. As referred above, with regard to territories (Federation, Republika Srpska, and Brcko District), each of the Entities and Districts has its own set of laws as well as those that are nationwide. The main factor is that the procedural laws regarding civil and criminal law within the country are considered to be similar in each entity and have been, for the most part, adopted unified throughout the country. Therefore, the legislative bodies can abolish the above adoption that was made in 2003 between the state-wide civil and criminal law of BiH. This can be one of the most problematic aspects, as there is not a strict rule and therefore the unified structure can easily be eradicated.

6. As previously mentioned, BiH is broken down into different jurisdictions with the following:

(1) The FBiH legal system covers the territory of the Federation and moves down to the ten Cantons formed within the FBiH. The Cantons are located in the following regions: Bihać, Orašje, Tuzla, Zenica, Goražde, Travnik, Mostar, Široki Brijeg, Sarajevo and Livno.
(2) The RS does not have Cantons but rather is defined by the respective districts which are the following: Banja Luka, Bijeljina, Doboj, Trebinje, and Istocno Sarajevo.
(3) Finally, Brcko District, which is situated in the city of Brcko, is not broken down further, as it is a small district within one city. It can be seen in the following picture of the structure of the country and how it is broken down:

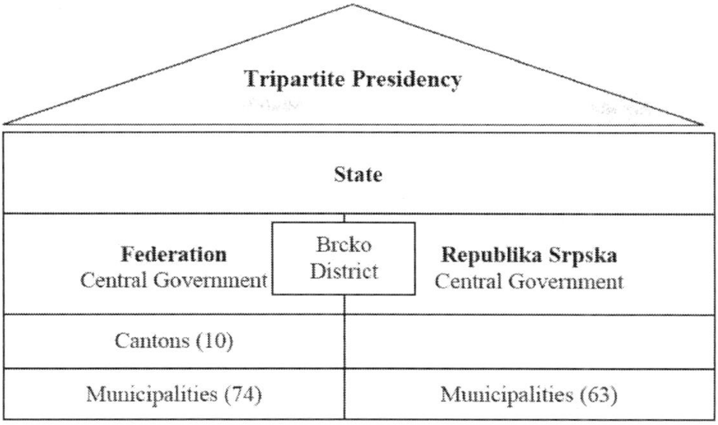

Source: BiH Document of World Bank Image: structure of BiH government.[2]

7. The Constitutional Court of BiH is part of a Frankenstein monster of a judicial system, cobbled together in post-war BiH from parts of the old Yugoslav system, the Dayton Peace Agreement and bits and pieces added by international donors (CIN 2008).[3] Unfortunately, this particular judicial system is something that has held back the country from further development compared to the other regional countries. BiH is composed of four distinct and autonomous legal systems that, in certain areas, do duplicate one another. The possibility of speedy trials in BiH is quite impossible due to the high number of cases and the complicated judicial system. The time frame of a case can range from two years or more before any decision is made and has even lasted up to ten years (depending on the case). Transparency International[4] found in a 2007 report that "the fact that there is no single structure of courts, has a significant impact on the work and efficiency of the judicial system." Due to this matter, the cases can take a long time before reaching a decision.

8. The system of the courts in the Federation Entity of Bosnia and Herzegovina (FBiH) and RS entities are as follows: Municipal (basic) cases may be appealed to the cantonal/district courts, and cantonal/district cases end in the Supreme Courts.[5] The Supreme Court is the final step, and the decision here may not be appealed further (unless the case pertains to Human Rights in which it may be appealed end up at the Constitutional Court of BiH). While in Brcko District, there are only two court systems, which are the ordinary/basic court and the appeals court. Only in particular circumstances may the appeal be submitted outside of the district. Finally, the Constitutional Court has jurisdiction over cases involving constitutional rights

2. *See* Govermental Structure of Bosnia and Herzegovina (2007).
3. *See* A cobbled Together Justice System (2007).
4. Also *see* Transparency International (2007).
5. A cobbled Together Justice System (2007).

(same as in entity but at the state level). Therefore, as well, the Constitutional Court has jurisdiction to overhear appeals that have a constitutional element from all of the lower courts (no matter the entity).

9. Considering that cases regarding sporting matters are often handled through ordinary courts, Sporting claims within the country are handled as ordinary claims due to the legal framework of such or through the respective Association/ Federation for the particular sport.

10. Ordinary Courts will dispute over the context of the claim, and in particular instances, it may have a different outcome than if it was submitted through the respective Federation. For example, if a player seeks overdue payables through the Football Federation of BiH, not a lot of sports clubs or athletes turn to the ordinary court due to a lack of a speedy trial to be able to understand the concept of the cases handled by the different stakeholders. The actual figure of how many cases is not as transparent, therefore the numbers are not available, but with the knowledge of the length of the trial and other abilities to claim a case, athletes or sports organizations will most likely return to the sports Associations/Federations for a solution, instead of the ordinary courts. One of the main reasons why ordinary courts may not be favored compared to sporting bodies is the lack of a speedy trial, and the second is the lack of knowledge and understanding of the sporting specificity in question.

11. In BiH, it does not have a well-organized online database for access to BiH jurisprudence. The database would allow for the studying of the decisions or claims, as well as helping build new cases by using previous precedents to assist on the particular matter. This is a setback to the legal system of BiH, which may play a big role in why the legal system of BiH is packed and backed up with cases that take ages to reach a decision. In precise, without a clear database and information that is accessible, it is difficult to shed light and educate others when working on a particular case or legal matter. This obstacle is simplified for those that have access to case reference numbers, therefore allowing them to access the case in some instances online. In regard to print access, it is mostly allowed to lawyers, educators and students, who may gain information on cases that can assist in pinpointing the actual substance and decision of the matter.

12. The organizational aspect of the country has far been outdated; therefore, all of this reflects on the legal complications in ordinary courts that may be seen throughout the country. It is more common that the person or organization taking the case forward making a claim will rather find a way to try to settle out of court or give up on taking the claim to court, mostly due to the time it would take for the particular case to be handled or decided upon. To understand the full extent of the impact of such, we can look at the key difference of such, if we compare to other countries, is drastic; for example, in the USA, we have the right to a speedy trial, while in BiH, the legal system is everything opposite of speedy. Unfortunately, the country is known for a prehistorical outdated system, in which most things are completed through print and paper, seldom online and through digital.

13. Therefore, the impact of digital development has resulted in most countries speeding up their administrative work, with numerous other positive factors, but in BiH, the digital world is still quite far behind. To develop the structure in sports, we must develop the country as a whole, this may be the most difficult task moving forward. Simplification of the system of the country will play a key role with respect to the development of sports and the country as a whole. Simplification and changes in the system is the first step to have any possibility to develop a clear system and the sports sector.

14. Throughout the history of BiH, we can see that the main complication for sports to move forward is the lack of governmental structure to be unified and to develop as does the rest of the western European countries. This is not always the worst-case scenario; if we look positively, there is much room for development and change, while in some countries, the line of development has currently reached its limitations.

§2. Sources of Sports Law

15. To fully understand the concept of Sports Law in a country, we must take into consideration the sources of sports law derived from the Country's Laws and sporting body regulations as a separate field of law. In BiH, not much can be found regarding the sources which define sports as a separate field of law or in particular support the sporting bodies in the legal framework other than a basic law guiding the sporting industry. The first aspect to understand is that BiH has a Law on Sport[6] at a national level, but the practice of such is broken down further by the entities and cantons by ordinary laws. Due to a lack of knowledge and education, the structure of sports law is still far from being functionally underdeveloped compared to regions around BiH, and therefore, we encounter complications that are still present today.

16. We must take into consideration that in Sports Law, the different practices have a core base, but the purpose is to tailor and define the already formed laws into one practice that governs the field of sport. If we take into consideration the sports industry around the world, we can conclude that it is a fast-growing industry. What most people do not recognize is the legal structure of sports that differs from that of a standard legal structure or that of ordinary laws. The lack of sports justice in a country plays a vital role in the development of sports. A unified system that does not tailor to sports will set back this industry because an athlete has a completely different status than an employee who works at the post office or any other industry due to the specificity of sports.

---

6. Law on Sport in Bosnia and Herzegovina (2017). *See also* the *Official Gazette of Bosnia and Herzegovina* No. 27/08 and the *Law on Amendments to the Law on Sports in Bosnia and Herzegovina* No. 102/09 and No. 66/16.

17. The sources of Sports Law, or those that govern the Sporting Industry in BiH, are a combination of laws, regulations and rulebooks derived from country laws, sports regulations and rulebooks that are in line with the above. Prior to stating the laws that may be encountered, we must understand where sports are derived from and on the governmental structure, who bears the responsibility of such. In the Law on Sport of BiH, Article 59[7] states the following:

> the competent authority for sports affairs at the level of Bosnia and Herzegovina is the Ministry of Civil Affairs of BiH, within which a special sector for sports is established.

18. Therefore, the highest authority on behalf of sports is the Ministry of Civil Affairs, which we will touch basis on further. Following the article previously mentioned, we must consider the same Law on Sport, in particular Article 60, which details the sector of sports and the work of such. In detail, it states that the jurisdiction of the sports sector is as follows:

(a) Organizing and managing the work of developing the sports strategy.
(b) Preparing proposals for long-term and annual sports development programs in BiH.
(c) Proposing the budget of the sports sector using gender-responsive budgeting.
(d) Preparation of proposals for regulations on the categorization of athletes and sports facilities.
(e) Preparation of regulations on keeping a register of legal and natural persons in the field of sports at the level of BiH.
(f) Determining the content and form of information systems on sports in BiH.
(g) Achieving cooperation with sports associations and other organizations and institutions.
(h) Defining the Strategy on the international level in the field of sports.
(i) Performing administrative, professional and other tasks in the field of sports in accordance with this law.

19. The highest power will be the Ministry of Civil Affairs within such, the sports sector shall have the ability to control the above-mentioned aspects. The Law in Sport is just a guideline, but we must consider the bodies overlooking the aspect of the sports industry. In coordination with the national Ministry of Civil Affairs, each entity, district or other administrative body (cantons or municipalities) shall have a separate Ministry of Sport on the particular level stipulated to work further within the respective jurisdiction.

20. The Ministry of Sport for Canton of Sarajevo was formed for the following reasons as stipulated in their rulebooks:[8]

7. *Ibid.*, at 11.
8. Ministry of Sport Canton of Sarajevo.

For determining and proposing policies in the field of sports, rest and recreation, (preparing, implementing, monitoring) the implementation of laws and regulations in the field of sports, organizing and participating in the organization of significant sports events and competitions, establishing and supervising the work of public institutions within their jurisdiction and other professional tasks related to the competence of the Ministry in this area.

21. While in the entity of Republika Srpska, the Ministry of Family, Youth, and Sport is a centralized authority with regard to the entity, unlike that of the Federation (Canon ministry) and this entity has a sector for sports, in line with the Ministry of Civil Affairs on national level. The RS Ministry of Family, Youth, and Sport[9] states that the following shall fall within their jurisdiction:

- creation of conditions for the development of sports at the level of the Republic and its legal regulation;
- determination of the Sports Development Strategy in the Republic and monitoring of the implementation of strategic and program tasks;
- realization of international cooperation independently or through joint bodies of BiH;
- preparation of short-term and long-term plans (Olympic cycle) for the development of sports in the Republic and programs for the development of sports and collection of funds for their realization;
- determination of criteria for their distribution and monitoring of the intended use of those funds;
- creating conditions for improving professional work;
- determining the condition of sports facilities and the need for new ones;
- creating assumptions for the use of sports facilities and grounds;
- registration of sports organizations and other organizations in sports;
- collection and processing of statistical data and management of overall informatics in sports;
- coordination of the work of branch sports associations of the Republic, city and municipality, as well as relevant bodies;
- supervision of the work of sports organizations and other organizations in sports;
- preparation of legal and by-laws within the competence of the Ministry and other tasks in accordance with the law.

22. There is always room to debate whether sports law is different and whether the cases should be handled through ordinary courts, as with any other claim. This particular debate has been ongoing, but with the fast-paced development of sports throughout the world, it is only natural that justice and laws be developed to tailor to such. Examples of such development may be seen in countries such as the United States of America, the United Kingdom, and Spain, which have personalized their education and practice in this area. It would be interesting to have a compared

9. Ministry of Family, Youth, and Sport Republic of Srpska.

analysis of the countries that have a tailored sports legal system in place with sports law at the core; compared to those that do not have a tailored system, it is hoped that such will widen to other countries.

23. Bearing in mind that BiH is split regarding entities and districts, the sports law structure is just as confusing as the judicial structure mentioned before. BiH has a nationally adopted Law on Sport, but what is important is how they are adopted by the entities and districts as well as further down the structure. Currently, the principles of law that govern sport are defined in national, entity and district, and Canton (where applicable). As defined in the Laws on Sport in Article 5(1), "Sport in BiH shall be organized in a decentralized manner with established rights and the competencies of BiH, Republika Srpska/Federation of BiH, and the Brcko District as well as other levels of administrative organization."[10] The confusion of the organized structure only leaves us with a headache of trying to understand where the jurisdiction lies between the national and ethnic in concern to particular sporting claims.

24. To try to further understand the circumstances between the different areas of the jurisdiction, it is important to mention that one of the obstacles is that the unified national Law on Sport does not in particular have to be adopted by the ethnic and canton regions. This setback is a sure way to guarantee that the legal system of BiH will never be truly unified and that all involved in sports will have to take into consideration the different levels and jurisdiction regions involved.

25. Next to the law on sport on the national level, we have Republika Srpska and Brcko District that have adopted a law on sport on this level. The Federation has not adopted such on an entity level but allowed for the Cantons to do so, therefore breaking down the regions and jurisdictions of the adopted law on sport instead of having one law that dictates all of the Cantons, we have broken it down significantly, which only promises for the law on sport not to function as a whole. The lack of a unified law system that must be adopted in other regions is a complication; therefore, ordinary laws have a further handle on the legal structure of sports in the country. This perplexity of a system has been one of the key factors for the obstruction of development of sports in the country; due to such, we see complications in the day-to-day work of the sports organizations (throughout the country).

26. Article 20 of the Law on Sport BiH[11] states that the sports club may be organized as a private or public-owned company, and further Article 20.2 states that the entities shall establish the details with regard to the founding of professional clubs. This is where we may see the first sign of complications in the matters of how sports organizations are registered. Our national laws allow for sports clubs to be organized as a company, but our entity, for example, in the Federation or Cantons, does not allow for such but rather only to be registered as an association. The lack of a wide country-adapted system, in which the national law takes precedent, shows us

10. *Supra* n. 6, at 11.
11. *Ibid.*, at 11 and 14.

that in the case of sports, the entity level has a higher power than the law governing on the national level and the lack of clarification which does not clearly state that the national law should take precedent compared to the entity but rather in most instances the national law dictates that the further definition of the particular article or regulation be defined on entity levels. This particular situation leaves us to feel that we are in three different countries instead of one.

27. Sport is governed not only by the Law on Sport BiH but also by ordinary laws such as Laws on Associations, Laws on Employment, Laws on Competition, etc. Another obstacle that may be seen is the fact that the Law on Sport in BiH does not detail all phases of sports organizations (employment, sponsorship, intermediaries, etc.,) but rather, it is distributed in the ordinary laws that are not subject to sports in general and then further defined between the laws in the particular jurisdiction of the country (entity, canton, etc.). This particular practice is not tailored to sports, therefore, the ordinary laws that are implemented in a sports organization are difficult to implement due to the special nature of sports and athletes. An example of this is Article 14 of the Law on Sport in BiH, which states:

> holders of sports activities in Bosnia and Herzegovina are legal and natural persons registered for performing sports activities in accordance with this Law, the Law on Associations and foundations of Bosnia and Herzegovina, laws on associations and foundations of entities, laws on entity sports, entity law and other levels of administrative organizing in Bosnia and Herzegovina.

28. Considering the various aspects of different laws, we must take into consideration the entities, as mentioned previously, with only the Federation of BiH (FBiH) not having a law on sport on the entity level. Therefore, it is much more complicated to find the right jurisdiction when entities do not apply a separate law as a whole, only the RS entity and Brcko District have, without the Federation (FBiH) adopting such. An example of the Law on Sport in RS and what it regulates can be found in Article 1,[12] which states the following:

> This law regulates the system of sports organization and other issues of importance for sports in the Republic of Srpska. General interest and programs in the field of sports, conditions for performing sports activity and activities, exercise of freedom of organization, rights and obligations of athletes, student sport activities, sports competitions and events, realization of international sports cooperation, sports facilities, professional work, prevention and suppression of violence and use of illicit means in sport, financing, informatics in sport, supervision and penal provisions.

29. The entity and district law details certain matters that may not be within the national law on sports and therefore is set to assist on matters that may pertain to the particular entity or district. The lack of an adopted law on sport at the level of

---

12. Zakon o Sportu Republika Srpska (October 2016).

the federation entity level leaves much room for complications and a lack of definition of the national law. Brcko District and RS have implemented the laws on their level, which can be seen as a simplification to the understanding of the Law on Sport on the national level.

30. The Federation entity consists of ten Cantons, and the laws on sports are left to each Canton to adopt; then, we leave room for potential complications since it is split in much smaller increments and does not have a definition on the entity level. This particular situation, as mentioned previously, has given too much space for complications and a lack of definition and strict implementations of laws on sports on the entity level throughout the country, leaving us to believe that the laws are not in favor of helping sports develop or to assist in the formation of such.

31. The fact that football is the most popular sport in BiH, such has seen the implementation of a law being adopted just for the matters of violence and prevention of such during sporting events. The major sport that is being watched and participated in BiH is football. Other sports may be seen as popular, but the numbers for football are far past the other top sports like basketball and handball. Due to the attraction of football to the fan base, we have seen many times that the partial fans at the stadium like to be part of a group considered to be the "ultras." Football has had the transition of violence within the stadiums and thus a new law was adopted to assist in the gathering of sporting events and violence that occur on stands. This law can expand to other sports, but it is known that it was solely adopted due to the footballing side. This Law was first mentioned in the Law on Sport BiH in Article 58, which defines that a separate law shall be formed for this particular reason.

32. The Zakon o Sprecivanju Nasilja na Sportskim Priredbima (2015)[13] or the English translation: "Law Against the Violence during Sporting Events," was adopted by the entities, but the entity of the Federation has not adopted this law but rather on the level of Cantons (similar to the adoption of Law on Sport on the entity, in the federation case, on the Cantonal level). This has been proven to be even more challenging since the canton levels have implemented their own system and, therefore, similar complications arise as the implementation of Law on Sport, where the level of jurisdiction is not strictly bound to entities but rather RS implement on entity level while FBiH on canton level. For example, there is a match to be held in the Canton of Tuzla, and the away fans from Sarajevo (Canton Sarajevo) are traveling to support their club in Tuzla. They have to be escorted by police, but the unique aspect of this is that at each canton, another police escort is awaiting to take the fans to Tuzla. It is not the police escort from Sarajevo Canton that escorts the fans all the way to Tuzla, but rather they escort the fans until they enter the next Canton, in which the police from such Canton will escort them further. This would

13. *Zakon o Sprecivanju Nasilja na Sportskim Priredbima* [Law on Violance during Sporting Events] (updated last 2015).

all be simplified if we had a unified law, at least in regard to sports that are on national level and under national association/federation umbrella, such as BiH Premier League Football.[14]

33. The fact that we have a competition that does not recognize boundaries played on national level, such as the premier football league, then there should be a system in which laws should apply, as the competition is not split by entity. If we look at the second division of the BiH league, it is split between RS and FBiH (Brcko District competes with RS because of the small number of clubs in this region) and therefore this competition can be an entity competition and entity laws shall have precedence.

34. With the above considerations of the National sources of Sports law, there must be a mention of the international laws that are recognized. As stated in the Law on Sport in BiH,[15] Article 4 of the International Scope states as follows:

> Sport in Bosnia and Herzegovina is based on the principles and standards established in the European Charter of Sport, the European Convention for the Protection of Human Rights and Fundamental Freedoms, the UN Convention on the Rights of the Child, the International Convention on Doping in Sport, European Convention on violence and misbehavior of spectators at sports events, Olympic the Charter, the Paralympic Charter, the rules of international sports associations, the European the Code of Sports Ethics, the Declaration on Sport, Tolerance and Fair Play, and the Lausanne Statement on organizing sports in Bosnia and Herzegovina.

35. To be able to further develop sports, it should be considered that the legal structure is set up differently. The countries in the region have a much more simplified structure of law in general and therefore it is easier to implement changes and adopt a law on sports that is unified for all in the country. Currently, due to the Daytona Agreement and the entities, BiH is having complications with a unified system and does not have the basis to adopt change until it starts from the top to the bottom of the country. With two entities and Brcko District not mentioning the three ethnic groups (Bosnian, Croatian, Serbian), it is always difficult to agree upon the standard for a law or even more for sports regulations.

It is as if you have three different nations under one roof with three different presidents. Another important factor can be an *unwritten rule* which has been established, for example, in the National Football team. If one coach is from the Bosnians (Muslim), then the following shall be from a different entity or ethnic group. The players called into the national team are usually mixed in ethnicities between Croats, Serbs, and Bosnians, making sure that all three are satisfied and cannot say that the national team is discriminating against any of the above. This has been an

14. The premier football league is unified (RS, FBiH, Brdsko District). The premier league used to be covered by entities and then at a particular stage was a playoff between the entity leagues for the winning of the national title. This is now the case only in the lower leagues (2nd, 3rd.).
15. *Ibid.*, at 11.

unwritten rule after the split of Yugoslavia, therefore making sure that all three are satisfied and that there would not be favoritism to one of the three.

§3. Bosnia and Herzegovina Specificity of Sport

36. Sport within BiH can be best seen through the regulations and acts adopted that have authority over such. The best example is Article 2[16] of the Law on Sport which defines what sport is and states the following:

(a) Sports activities and games organized for the purpose of achieving sports achievements according to established rules (sports competitions and sports events).
(b) Sports activities and games that are organized with the aim of improving health or recreation (sports recreation, sports for all).
(c) Sports activities organized for persons with disabilities.
(d) Organized school and university sports.

Article 2 dictates how sport is defined and those they may fall within laws. The complication we sometimes have with the specificity of sport is the understanding of what may fall within the scope of such. The majority of sports that are considered recreational, amateur, school competition, and professional will fall within this law. Sport is a crucial aspect within a community and one that can impact in a very positive way or at least help the community with regard to living a healthier lifestyle, especially if we are not considering such just for the amateur and professional aspect.

37. Specificity in sports has been much-debated with regard to what may be decided upon by the ordinary courts and what may be regulated only by the sporting organizations. An important and first case to show the specificity of sport was in Walrave & Koch.[17] This case showed and confirmed that the European Union (EU) Law did not apply to rules of the game or as mentioned in the case, of "sporting interest" on the basis that such rules had nothing to do with the economic activities to which the EC Treaty relates.[18] In other words and as mentioned in the case, European law only applies to "economic activities" within the overall meaning of Article 2 of the Treaty.[19] We can see a trend where ordinary courts have applied the specificity of sport and in other circumstances, they have made a ruling on the decision of such.

38. It is still unclear in BiH what is ruled upon in the ordinary courts or what must be submitted within the sporting federations, associations, and/or Court of

16. *Ibid.*
17. *Walrave & Koch v. Association Union Cycliste Internationale "Walrave"* delivered on Dec. 12, 1974, Netherlands (European Court).
18. *See*: *Walrave & Koch v. Association Union Cycliste Internationale "Walrave"* para. 4.
19. *Ibid.*, para. 8.

Arbitration for Sport (CAS). Within the scope of sports, it has been interesting to watch the development of CAS and the regulations within the respective sports according to the international federations. The legal system in Europe and the such can differ from country to country, but the new adoption of sports law or similar regulations of such has proven the beginning of a regulated industry that was previously shoved into the regulations of other industries.

39. In BiH, this is still left unclear, as in most circumstances due to the lack of a more defined law on sport, the ordinary courts still take on the consideration of making a ruling. There have been abundant cases in which the sports federations/associations may decide through disciplinary proceedings, but the party turned to the ordinary courts in hopes that the outcome may be clearer and more simplified. For example, the employment contracts of athletes in BiH are under the jurisdiction of Employment law but have the ability to be submitted to the sports federations/associations. In most circumstances, the athletes will turn to ordinary courts, and the courts will uphold decisions, even though the sporting sector may have a procedure in place for resolution.

40. There must be a distinctive procedure to be able to implement in BiH to simplify the current complicated judicial system that has been adopted. The factor is that sports and other industries are split between the jurisdictions of their countries. The power of decision on matters is sometimes left at the discretion of the claimant submitting the claim. Not in all instances will the claimant have more options of the procedure between ordinary courts and disciplinary proceedings from the respective federations or associations. At times, the claimant may have to decide a patch in which the laws set forth may be in his or her favor and, due to other circumstances, that may impose the decision process of where one may submit or lodge a claim.

Part I. The Legal Framework

§1. Public Law and Fundamental Rights

41. The Law on Sport in BiH[20] entails the rights of stakeholders and persons (s) participating in sports within the country. Public Law, regarding the connection between individuals and the government, can be seen through the regulations and laws set within the country. The complication arises when the governmental institutions break down the regulations according to the Federation, Brcko District, and Republics Srpska, which is further broken down into the Canton levels of the Federation. As mentioned previously, the need for a unified system impacts the sports stakeholders and individuals participating in the sporting sector.

42. The fundamental rights of the stakeholders (organizations) and the individuals are set and regulated accordingly. That said, individuals and organizations could participate in sports. The only right that can be seen as a complication is the organizational aspect of the country's split. According to Public Law, the rights of the organizations and individuals are set and do not deviate from the ability to participate in such. However, complications arise when we analyze the breakdown of the laws and the right to seek relief or justice on behalf of such.

43. A player has the full fundamental rights as any other person(s) in the country. As stipulated in Article 37.2 of the Law on Sport in BiH:

> An athlete has all the civil rights set out in the Constitution and laws of Bosnia and Herzegovina, entity constitutions and laws, and other regulations at other levels such as administrative organizations, and the provisions that are set by this law as well as the entity laws on the sport.

Consequently, the player is protected concerning the highest level of the Constitution and has the full fundamental rights as any other person within the country. Considering the above, Article 39 details the rights of the player that are different from those of Article 37. An athlete has the right to the following as stipulated in the above Article 39, which are the following:

(a) Be protected from all kinds of mental and physical violence that may endanger the freedom of human beings and sporting integrity, health, and

20. *See* Law on Sport in Bosnia and Herzegovina, 2017.

> sporting dignity, *Has the right to use sports facilities and equipment, professional work, and health care services following regulations governing it, and participates in representative selections based on free will.*

44. The player also has obligations to which he/she must abide. Law on Sport in BiH defines such obligations within Article 40; all players must:

(a) Respect the rules of behavior for the particular sport.
(b) Regularly train and participate in the competition.
(c) Respect the rules of the game, the spectators, and officials.
(d) Must preserve the reputation of the sporting organization.
(e) Must corporate with health services and other officials to make sure that he/she is not using illegal substances (WADA).

45. Just as players have certain rights and obligations, similar is also set out for Sports Clubs. Regarding obligations and as mentioned in Article 6 of Law on Sport in BiH:

> the club must make sure that there is no discrimination against players, that the club does follow the rights of the players, allows for the players to have medical insurance or coverage, does not discriminate towards the players, allow them for proper equipment, training or competition.[21]

46. The fundamental rights of person(s) in general and not descriptive only to the athletes are stipulated initially in the Constitution of BiH in Article 4 which stipulates that:

> Services. Capital. and Persons. There shall be freedom of movement throughout Bosnia and Herzegovina. Bosnia and Herzegovina and the Entities shall not impede full freedom of movement of persons, goods, services, and capital throughout Bosnia and Herzegovina. Neither Entity shall establish controls at the boundary between the Entities.

Bosnia and Herzegovina, set out by the above regulations, allow for the freedom of movement and other jurisdictions should not impose any acts against such. As mentioned in the above paragraphs, the jurisdictional split does in fact impose complications in regard to the legal aspect and that of procedure, but with regard to movement, there must be freedom of such. Within the scope of public law, the Constitution plays the highest role in the implementation between the individual person(s) and the government. The rights of individuals within BiH are supported by similar standards to those within Europe and worldwide but to grasp the full extent,

21. *Ibid.*, at 11 and 21.

another article to consider within the Constitution of BiH[22] shall be Article 3. The particular article is with regard to the Enumeration of Rights and such article states the context of the following:

(a) The right to life.
(b) The right not to be subjected to torture or to inhuman or degrading treatment or punishment.
(c) The right not to be held in slavery or servitude or to perform forced or compulsory labor.
(d) The rights to liberty and security of person.
(e) The right to a fair hearing in civil and criminal matters, and other rights relating to criminal proceedings.
(f) The right to private and family life, home, and correspondence.
(g) Freedom of thought, conscience, and religion.
(h) Freedom of expression.
(i) Freedom of peaceful assembly and freedom of association with others.
(j) The right to marry and to found a family.
(k) The right to property.
(l) The right to education.
(m) The right to liberty of movement and residence.

Each person has the above rights and protection when in scope of individuals and therefore of athletes. Even when traveling between the different jurisdictions within BiH, each individual shall receive the rights as stipulated within the Constitution and no particular body or authority may act differently than as stipulated by such.

I. Right to Practice Sport (If It Exists)

47. The right to participate in sports is defined throughout BiH, and discrimination is prohibited in any sport. The particular laws may be seen in the Law on Sport in BiH, and throughout the articles of the Law, we can conclude that athletes have the right to practice and participate in sports. With this in mind, there are still some irregularities in the aspects of men and women competing in professional sports.

48. If we look at football, it has been mostly seen as a men's sport, and although women are allowed and have clubs to participate in, we still need more equality when it comes to the community accepting women within such a sport. There have been cases where women were not allowed to play because it was considered a men's sport. Although the community might have opinions on such participation, the laws and regulations do not allow for discrimination on any basis or the ability to participate in such.

---

22. Consitution of BiH, Law No. 25/09 of Mar. 26, 2009 in Sarajevo, BiH.

49. The adoption of the Law on Gender Equality in Bosnia and Herzegovina (LGE-BiH)[23] in 2010 stipulates the laws that allow for equality of person(s) within the country. The laws were another factor that gave protection for equality as it was implemented in the Constitution, Law on Sport and other laws and regulations deemed relevant to the right to practice sport within the country. Article 2 of the LGE-BiH states that the following rights are given:

(1) Persons of male and female sex shall be equal.
(2) Full gender equality shall be guaranteed in all spheres of society, including but not limited to education, economy, employment and labor, social and health protection, sport, culture, public life and media, regardless of marital and family status.
(3) Discrimination on the grounds of gender and sexual orientation is prohibited.
(4) Discrimination, in terms of this Law, shall not be considered introduction, adoption and implementation of temporary special measures aiming to remove existing inequality, promote equality and protection of gender equality.
(5) Discrimination on grounds of gender shall not be considered a norm, criteria or practice which can be justified by achieving a legal goal, proportionate to taking necessary and justified measures.

Article 2 of the LGE-BiH allows us to understand the protection of equality, i.e., the right to be able to participate in sports no matter the gender. This is important to highlight as it is still known that in sports around the world, there is no equality of the same treatment for women with regard to sports equality like men's sports. The laws and regulations have protected such with regard to equal treatment, but it is widely known that the community has some lack of the same implementation even within the scope of the sporting organizations. Girls and women do have rights, but it is important to find the best ways to educate and implement the same rights within the community, no matter the gender.

Under the same LGE-BiH[24] articles, there is a mention of equality with regard to Sports and Culture and this is stipulated in Article 19 with the following:

(1) Everyone has equal rights and opportunities to participate in and have access to sport and cultural life regardless of gender.
(2) The relevant authorities, institutions and juristic persons are required to undertake all possible measures to prevent discrimination on the grounds of gender and to ensure equal opportunities for:
    (a) access to branches of sport or culture;
    (b) the development and provision of support for individual branches of sport or culture;
    (c) the granting of community awards for outstanding achievement in sport and culture within the same branch of sport or culture.

23. Law on Gender Equality in Bosnia and Herzegovina (2010).
24. *Ibid.*, on 24.

Men and women shall have the right to participate in sports, and they must have the protection of doing so according to the laws stipulated.

50. The Law on Sport in BiH, particularly Article 37,[25] regulates an athlete's rights and the ability to participate in sports. As stated, all athletes have the same rights as any other person in BiH and must comply with the laws and accords to the Constitution of BiH, laws and accords to the Entity level, and other regulations that may be deemed relevant to the athletes. Furthermore, the regulations within the Law on Sport dictate that persons have the right to practice or participate in sports. Therefore, the articles within the Law allow for the complete protection of such athletes (Bosnian, resident or international participating in BiH).

II. Freedom of Association

51. The Law on Sport BiH, entity or district laws, and Canton Law on Sport regulate the Association of Sports within the country, allowing sports or clubs to register as an association according to the laws on such. An essential factor to take into consideration is that the Law in Sport on the BiH level states the aspect of how organizations can be registered. However, this is further broken down by the Regulations, Laws on Entity/jurisdiction, and Canton Level. Considering this, we must consider that parts of the country are split according to the jurisdiction level of Entity, District, and Cantons; in essence, clubs or sports bodies must be registered as Associations. The registration of clubs as Associations was a unified law that governed throughout the country, but recently the changes in RS and the regulations in this particular entity, the update allows for clubs to be registered as companies. Until recently, the regulations, laws, and Ministry of Justice only allowed the sports organizations to be seen as associations, but the entity of Republika Srpska recently adopted a new entity law on sports, which allows for sports organizations to be registered as associations or companies. This collaborates with the previously mentioned paragraphs where there needs to be a more straightforward, unified way throughout the country, which is an imbalance considering that in most sports, clubs compete on a national level, not just on the entity level.

52. With regard to the Laws on Association and Foundations, to be able to register an Association, the following is stated under Article 9:[26]

> the association can be founded by at least three founders. The founders of the association can be physical persons who are citizens of Bosnia and Herzegovina and foreigners who have in Bosnia and Herzegovina place of residence or legal entities registered in Bosnia and Herzegovina. Association can establish mutual natural and legal entities, but the number of founders cannot be less than three.

25. *See* Art. 12 Law on Sport BiH (2017).
26. Laws on Association and Foundations ("Official Gazette of BiH," Nos. 32/01, 42/03, 63/08, 76/11 and 94/16).

Most sports collectives or clubs are organized within this aspect as an Association and given the right to be able to function under the Laws of Association of BiH, Entity, District or Cantons. The Laws are set forth with regard to the formation and work of the Association and then further detailed through the laws, such as the laws on sport depending on the related jurisdiction.

53. As stipulated in the Law in Sport of RS (Zakon o Sportu RS ("Sl. glasnik RS," br. 79/2020)) [2], Article 43 states:

> "In order to perform sports activities, a sports organization can be established as an association or as a business company." This Article stipulates that sports organizations can be organized as companies, allowing the clubs to be privately owned, like other businesses in different industries, unlike the other entity or Brcko District, which only allows for the organizations to be considered associations and does not give the same flexibility.

54. The structure for the Brcko District and the Federation of sports organizations are legally formed as associations, with assemblies, boards of directors, and administrations composed within. The fact that the sports organizations are formed as associations means that the club cannot be privately owned, and there are no ways to own stock of the club, as there are certain circumstances of ownership of sports clubs or stocks in other countries. The Law on Association and Foundation for the Federation[27] and the Brcko District[28] regulate how sports organizations should be registered as associations in a particular jurisdiction.

55. In 2013, the Football Club "FK Sarajevo" was the first to have an investor within its structure. This was the ground breaking first step to reform how clubs should be managed. Although the club can only be registered as an association, the legal framework allowed the owner to buy the voting rights of the Assembly. As a result, FK Sarajevo made the first emission for the public to buy voting rights and membership within the Assembly; considering that the foreign investor funded the most money and met the emission criteria, he received 91% of the total voting rights of the Assembly. Therefore, although the club was not under the ownership of the foreign investor, the investor still could make the critical decisions as he had the majority voting rights in the Assembly.[29] Considering Article 16 of the Laws on Association and Foundations of BiH, the assembly members all have equal rights in deciding on the Association unless stipulated differently within the statutes of the Association.

56. The Law on Associations and Foundations FBiH Article 18 states that the rights of the assembly members are as follows:

---

27. *Ibid.*, at 26.
28. The Law on Association and Foundation Brcko District (2002).
29. Assembly is the highest level of any Association; therefore, with a majority seats in the Assembly, a member can have the controlling voting rights.

(a) Adopting the Statute, amending the Statute, and other acts specified in the Statute.
(b) Deciding on merger, division, termination of work, the establishment of other legal entities, as well as, other status changes of the Association.
(c) The appointment and dismissal of members of the board of directors, if such an association exists.
(d) Adopting reports prepared by the board of directors, if such an association body exists.
(e) Deciding on any other matter, not within the competence of the other bodies of the Association.

Considering the above article, the critical aspects of deciding within an association are reflected in the members of the Assembly. Furthermore, considering that FK Sarajevo allowed for the emission into the Assembly by bidding for voting rights and as stipulated in internal statutes and documents, the Assembly received a member with the majority of voting rights by acquiring the most amount of voting rights from the amount of cash submitted for the bid of such. Therefore, the club allowed for an investor to be admitted through the ownership of the majority voting rights of the club.

57. The reform of FK Sarajevo did not just stop there; another football club in the FBiH entity achieved a similar reform. In 2017/2018, the football club "NK Celik" had a similar effect; a foreign investor bought the majority voting rights in the Assembly of the club and therefore had the right to make critical decisions. However, the protection of the majority rights holder is not the same as if the foreign investor or owner of the voting rights had the fundamental right to privately own the club or have stock ownership. This is one step forward in investment into sports organizations when the ability to register is only as an association, while we are still waiting for sports organizations in the RS Entity to register as companies, as per the new Law adopted for Law in Sport RS.

58. The provisions of Article 31 of the Law on Sport BiH stipulate the following:

> that Legal Entities-Sports Associations are founded and organized freely and are independent in the exercise of their rights and obligations, following this Law, the Entity Laws on Sport, the Law on Associations and Foundations of *Bosnia and Herzegovina, the Entity Laws on associations and foundations.*[30]

The Law defines that all shall be organized freely, but they must abide by the regulations of the laws stipulated above. Depending on the location of the sports organization or club, it has to abide by the laws of Associations, entities, districts, and Laws on Sports BiH. For example, if the club or sport is located in the RS entity, they must first abide by the Laws on Sport in BiH, then the Law on Sport of RS.

---

30. *See* Art. 31 of Law on Sport in Bosnia. *and Herzegovina* (2017).

59. We must take an insight into Article 5 of the BiH Law on Association and Foundations which stipulates the right that an association registered in RS shall be free to carry out activities or acts in the federation "without any additional administrative conditions" (BiH laws on Associations and Foundations). The article stated above gives clarity in regard to when a club is registered in one entity, it shall have the freedom to carry out activities in another entity. Such as in a way that the registration shall be carried out by shifting the information from the decision of the registration of the Association registered (Article 26 BiH laws on Associations and Foundations).[31] The freedom to carry out activities in different parts of the country in concern to entity allows one step closer for the sports clubs to be unified, but due to the registration of the particular club or association/company, it must abide by the laws of where the particular club or organization is registered in the legal means.

60. According to this provision above, and taking into account the provisions of the Law on Associations and Foundations at the state, federal and cantonal levels, the establishment of clubs and associations is accessible under the conditions and restrictions laid down by these laws, and for the club to exercise its right to participate in national leagues fulfillment of the requirements of the Rulebook of the competent federations (e.g., the Rulebook of the NS BIH on the status and transfer of players of the NS BIH, which regulates the licensing of football clubs for participation in leagues at the level of BiH).

61. Also, under the Law on Sport BiH, it is clearly stated throughout the Law that the sports organizations have the freedom to become an association or associate as a sport collective. For example, the football club FK Sarajevo used to be part of the Sarajevo Sports Association (SSA), where numerous sports were under the same umbrella. This assisted in making sure that all sports were grouped and had unified rights toward the sports associations. For example, under this umbrella, the SSA had different associations like football, basketball, track, and field. This allowed associations to join under one roof, therefore moving forward in developing a bigger brand. Similar organizations may be seen in Europe, such as Barcelona, Spain.

III. Personality Rights

62. In the Law on Sport BiH, no particular article or regulation defines personality rights, image rights, or similar rights. The special protection of athletes for using their image or rights for marketing/merchandising purposes on a national level has yet to be discovered. It is recognized in many countries abroad that athletes have separate agreements or negotiations involving using their branding rights for the benefit of the stakeholder. Such would be in consideration of athletes that are paid for participating in a particular sport. However, it has been influential for athletes to gain monetary gain by exploiting their personality rights and the ability to generate income outside of just playing the sport.

31. *See* Art. 26 IV *Law on Associations and Foundations of BiH.*

63. As mentioned above, the national Law on Sport does not stipulate any regulation to such, but when we look at the level under, we can find a different situation. In the Law on Sport RS adopted in 2020, the articles mention an athlete's right to his personality rights/image rights. The particular Article that defines the protection of personality rights in the Law on Sport RS is Article 29, which states the following:

> A professional athlete and a sports organization, when concluding an employment contract or a sports engagement contract, may separately agree on the provision of one-time benefits to the athlete, namely:
>
> (1) Compensation for the conclusion of the contract.
> (2) Fee for using the image of an athlete.
> (3) Monetary and other awards for a notable contribution to the achieved result.
> (4) The total one-time fees referred to in paragraph 1 of this Article may amount to a maximum of one-half of the total amount of the contract.

64. Article 29 of Law on Sport RS[32] clearly defines the possibility for the fee of the image or personality right of the athlete. It is essential to understand that the Law only allows for a one-time payment, not a reoccurring situation. Also, if we look at item 2 of the same Article, the total amount is limited, with it being a maximum of one-half of the total amount of the initial employment contract of the athlete. Although regulated, unlike the other entities and National Law, it is still stipulated and limited to a particular amount.

65. Athletes, Clubs, Businesses and Organizations have been having difficulty entering into agreements that regulate personality rights on the Federation and Brcko levels due to the lack of the existing Law. As a result, there have been cases in which the organization or sports stakeholders had to find ways to prove what personality rights mean and how much the club or organization has benefited from using such personality rights. Unfortunately, the lack of regulation in particular jurisdictions is called a "grey area," where there is no law to punish organizations for using such. However, the same applies to the enforcement of said agreements. This still needs to be regulated on the country level which leaves room for interpreting said fees for such rights.

66. Regarding Sports Bodies, such as the BiH Football Association (FA), we have an exciting aspect of personality rights. It is essential to mention that the FA distributes the unified employment contract to be used by the clubs; in such a contract, there is a mention of image rights and the club's total ability to use the rights of the athlete as a whole. This leaves the athlete only able to market and use the

32. *See* Law on Sport od Republika Srpska (Official Gazzete Nos. 4/2002, 66/2003, 73/2008, 102/2008).

personality/image rights toward the club and may not be able to generate added income from companies wishing to exploit their image for monetary gain. The employment contract supplied by the FA will be looked into in detail under such section further in the insert. To understand the fundamental aspect, athletes worldwide have the discretion to allow the clubs to have a certain right to their image/personality, but a certain percentage would be left for the athlete's discretion. The importance of the ability of athletes to have part of the personality rights is that they may be able to gain monetary gain from companies that inquire about marketing them. One such pillar can be seen in David Beckham and his monetary gain outside of the pitch.

§2. Governmental Conditions and Permits (Quotas, Work Restrictions)

67. Regarding the governmental conditions, it can be clearly derived from the above text that the Association must be registered as an association and clearly stipulated within the laws the way to consider the registration. With regard to governmental conditions, the sports organization must be registered with the Federal Ministry or the Cantonal Ministry depending on the location. Regarding work restrictions, the critical factor is that the associations are to work under such regulations and must abide by the Laws on Employment stipulated for a person(s) employed within the organization. As stated in the Laws on Associations and Foundations BiH Article 4:

> It is not permitted to obtain, directly or indirectly, profit or any other material gain generated through the activities of the association or foundation to founders, members of the association, members of the managing bodies, responsible persons, employees or donors.[33]

This may be seen as a limitation, as this article clearly defines that the associations are not permitted to obtain profit for material gain, which, in some essences, we can consider a work limitation of the Association.

68. In regard to athletes and sports professionals who are considered foreigners, the only governmental permit or condition is that athletes and sports professionals must have a work permit from the competent state authority and register with the entity ministry responsible for sports or in Brcko District, the competent authority of BiH. The critical fact to consider is that the work permit can only be issued for one year and must be extended. Therefore, if the athlete has an employment contract with a sports organization, they must re-apply for the work permit every additional year.

69. To apply for a work permit, the athlete must also obtain a visa for their stay in BiH. The visa is the first part of the process, which the sports organization applies

33. *See* Art. 4 *Law on Associations and Foundations BiH.*

through an official invitation letter to the athlete approved by the Office for the Service of Foreigners. After the visa is granted, the athlete will take the next step with the sports organization to obtain the work permit. Important to reiterate again that such has to be renewed on an annual basis.

70. To understand the quota of those applying for work permits in BiH, we must look at Article 64[34] of the Law on the Movement and Residence of Foreigners and Asylum, which defines the ability to set a quota on the number of work permits given to a particular branch of industry and not directly defining that of sports. The Council of Ministers is the deciding body concerning the particular quotas for foreigners and work permits in the particular industry. Thus far, there has not been a prohibition or quota limit for that athlete and the ability to apply for work permits.

71. Due to the specificity of sport, the process of obtaining the visa and work permit can impact the duration until such paperwork is completed and approved. It has been common, especially in football, that certain athletes could not automatically participate with the sporting organization due to the wait for the work permit and visa. We must also consider the different international regulations stipulating that an employment contract cannot be subject to the approval of a work permit. Nevertheless, the process has successfully allowed foreigners to compete in sports organizations in BiH; the duration of the procedure and paperwork may be the only burden.

72. Once the athlete obtains the work permit and visa, they are protected concerning discrimination and the ability to participate. All athletes who receive the right regarding the work permit can participate in the sports organization by which the athlete is registered and employed.

§3. Tax Law Applied to Sport

73. The fundamental problem for the significant development of Professional Sports in BiH is, among other things, that the engagement of professional players is equal to that of workers in any other sector and industry. It is essential to emphasize that the rates of contributions and related taxes from the employment relationship based on the work are also applied to professional players. Bearing in mind the high tax and contribution rates of approximately 70%, it is impossible for clubs on the territory of BiH to negotiate salaries with players that are adequate for their quality and abilities.

For example, if the club contracts a salary of BAM 10,000 with the player, it is obliged to pay an additional approximately 70% of the stated amount.

74. Certain solutions exist in local laws, which apply to the so-called professional occupations (not yet considered for athletes/players), whereby the associated

34. *Law on the Movement and Residence of Foreigners and Asylum* ("Official Gazzet BiH" Nos. 88/2015 and 34/2021).

taxes and contributions are calculated on the legally determined fixed so-called lump-sum part of the income, which is characterized as a salary (e.g., BAM 1,000). In contrast, only profit tax is calculated on the remaining amount at 10%. Therefore, the eventual regulation of the status of professional athletes in this context would most certainly lead to the improvement of sports since it would enable the payment of higher fees to professional athletes for their engagement, which would ultimately result in the mapping of BiH as a significantly more attractive sports market.

75. When we look with regard to taxation in BiH, different categories are part of taxation, such as follows:

(1) Value-added taxes:
- Tax on profit.
- Income tax.
- Property tax.
- Social security contributions paid by employer and employee.
- Excise (luxury) tax.

These are some of the main taxations which are adopted in the entities and Brcko District. In some cases, the tax may be regulated differently with regard to the percentage to be paid depending on the entity or Brcko District. As mentioned in the previous paragraph, due to high taxation, sporting organizations have considered other ways to get out of paying taxes by signing players to amateur contracts or service agreements in which the tax rate is three times less than that of an employment contract. The sports organization cannot follow the Balkan region (Croatia, Serbia, Slovenia) in regard to sports development because of the high tax for salaries. The higher the tax, the less of the net the player may receive due to the limit on profit the sports organization is able to obtain. It has been seen where sports organizations have made double contracts for athletes by using sister companies or similar thereof. Even in this aspect, the double contract does not give legal protection to the athlete due to the second contract.

76. Another aspect to consider is that any added salary or income from the same organization for the employed athlete must be paid 70% of the added profit. In addition, a club that pays for the accommodation of their employed athlete must pay an additional tax on the amount given in accommodation. Another factor is that sports organizations found ways to pay athletes in cash, stating a very small amount of salary on the employment contract and the rest paid in cash. Paying an athlete in cash from the sports club is illegal and therefore leaves much room for the club to have penalties, and the athletes are not protected from payment. These factors all show the difficulty the tax system has caused on employment in general as well as the development of sports.

77. Considering that employment taxation for professional athletes is under regulations for all employees on taxation and contributions, we must examine both laws. The first is the Income Tax Law split between entities of BiH[35] and how it is defined, primarily how it is implemented concerning sporting organizations. The second is the Law on Contributions[36] in FBiH; this applies to both entities but is stipulated within the particular entity's and District's laws. For this example, we will review the Income Tax Law of FBiH, which directly states under Article 2 that the following person(s) shall be considered liable for income tax:

(1) The taxpayer of income tax is a resident of the Federation and a non-resident who generates income as follows: a resident who earns income within the territory of the Federation and outside the territory of the Federation:
  (1) A non-resident engaged in an independent activity through a permanent place of business in the territory of the Federation.
  (2) Non-resident engaged in independent activity in the territory of the Federation.
  (3) A non-resident who derives income from the territory of the Federation from movable and immovable property, copyrights, patents, licenses, investment of capital, or any other activity that results in income that is taxable under this Law.

(2) When more natural persons collectively generate income, the taxpayer is each natural person, in particular, for his share, which he generates in the income thus generated.

(3) For this Law, a resident of the Federation shall be considered:
A natural person residing in the territory of the Federation, a natural person who resides on the territory of the Federation continuously or intermittently for 183 or more days in any tax period, a natural person residing in the Federation and, based on performing an independent activity outside the territory of the Federation, receives income from the federal budget or the budget of Bosnia and Herzegovina.

(4) For this Law, a non-resident shall be considered a natural person who has been staying in the territory of the Federation for less than 183 days.

(5) Permanent place of business means the place where the activity is registered.

78. Another aspect to consider is the athletes with scholarships or amateur contracts, mainly used for youth athletes still in school or athletes competing in amateur leagues. The amateur contract, in particular, has its limitations and thus is not used in professional sports organizations for profit but rather for the right to participate in the sport. Unfortunately, due to the high taxes, sports organizations are not protected in keeping their talented athletes unless they have an employment contract. Therefore, an athlete may leave at any point, unlike the crucial aspect of an employment contract.

---

35. *Income Tax Law FBiH* ("Official Gazzet BiH" 10/08, 9/10, 44/11, 7/13 and 65/13).
36. *Law on Contribution FBiH* ("Official Gazzet BiH" No. 35/98).

§4. Principles of Tort Law

79. As stated in the Oxford Handbook of American Sports Law, "conduct that harms other people or their property is generally called tort."[37] Tort law can be defined as private or public wrongdoing. In Sports Law, we may find different ways in which we can define tort law. The Bosnian Legal System, therefore, has different segments that are considered part of tort law. Let us look at tort law in sports. Some of the different ways we may define such can be the following: Negligence, spectator injuries, wrongful death, malpractice in sports, sports officials, workers' compensation, and insurance. Considering that sports is a growing industry and the vast circumstances that arise, we can all define them under tort law. The different person(s) that can seek relief under tort law may be athletes, spectators, and other persons involved in the sporting activity or the sports club, who could be liable or can seek relief.

80. The definition of tort is not clearly defined under the national Law on Sport but rather in a separate law, that is, the Law on Offenses BiH,[38] which is not directly defined under the name of tort law within the country but somewhat under the Law on Offenses. As defined by the Law on Offense, Article 2 definition of the offense is as follows:

(a) Misdemeanors represent violations of public policy or regulations on economic and financial operations established by Law or other regulations for which the characteristics of the offense are determined and for which sanctions are prescribed.
(b) The offense may be committed by act or omission.
(c) The negligence of the perpetrator is sufficient to hold the perpetrator liable for the offense unless the provisions of the offenses stipulate that he will be punished for the act done solely with intent.
(d) Natural and legal persons may commit offenses.
(e) Attempting to commit an offense is not punishable.

As we can gather from the above, this is the definition that is proposed even in events concerning sports in BiH.

81. Negligence, as defined by US Legal, "is the failure to abide by a level of care that a reasonable person would follow to avoid unforeseeable harm." For example, it is difficult to say that an athlete on the pitch during a football match may be held accountable for the injury of the opponent, as both parties had agreed in consent to be part of such sport, in which contact may be part of the sport. We have seen instances where a player has deliberately caused harm to another player, and with severity, this can directly impact the decision of whether the player can be held responsible. Can a boxer be held responsible for negligence under tort law by

37. *M.McCann, Oxford Handbook of American Sports Law* (2012).
38. *Law on Offense in BiH* (Prnjavorac, 2015).

knocking out the opponent? This may be too wide of a question for us to answer directly without considering all the circumstances.

82. There have been cases in which the athlete has acquired a claim against the other party for negligence, even in the instances above. This is all about interpreting the event and the cause of the injury and negligence. "In both professional and amateur contact sports, athletes consent to some physical contact, but courts do not find that participants consent to contact that goes outside the bounds of the game" (Jrank Law).[39] As we can gather, it is pretty essential to understand what falls under "*outside the bounds of the game.*" For example, a football player during a match on purpose injures a player to the extent that it can be seen that he did not act in the essence of the game but could not instead take due care to avoid such injury; this may be seen as negligence.

83. Another example may be if the boxer punches the opponent after the bell rings, we can gather that the person who punched the opponent may be negligent under such Law (Law on Offense). Law on Offense in BiH is similar to that of most countries regarding stipulating the definition and the ability to hold a person responsible.

I. Civil Liability

84. In civil liability, a party must pay for damages that may have occurred, and similar can be seen in sports. A direct example of such can be spectator injuries (but not subject just to spectators). In some cases, not just hold a person liable, but in most circumstances, the organizer of the event may be held liable for the cause of injury. Article 2 (2) of the Law on Offenses states that a natural and private person may be held accountable in cases of offense or negligence. Spectator injuries can be vast and difficult to put into one section, considering what we must consider. The failure to supervise and organize the event and lack of due care may raise a claim concerning tort or offense, depending on the claim's facts.

85. For example, during a football match in which FK Sarajevo played against FK Sloboda, the home spectator was injured in the ultra-stand by stepping on a firework/flare; he had significant injuries to his foot during the start of the match.[40] The fan sued the club for reimbursement for the negligence of the club, holding the club responsible, as it is the event organizer. The club used the defense that the plaintiff knew of the possibility of flares (fireworks) because the spectator stands in which the plaintiff was located were known for fireworks and flares. Thus, he should have taken due care to attend a stand that was not of the ultras and one which had no use of flares. Another defense was to show that the plaintiff was known to help participate in the flares as the ultra-stand was held by a joint group of fans called Horde Zla.

39. Jrank Law, Tort Law in Sports.
40. *Ensar Jusufovic v. FK Sarajevo*, delivered in 2019, Sarajevo Canton Court (Civil).

The court applied Res ipsa loquitur[41] as applicable in this case, holding that the lack of caution by the club to restrict the flares in the stand was directly involved in the negligence and thus are liable as such. The court held the club liable and believed it had control of the cause of the injury and that the club should have taken further precautions to avoid such an event. This is considered under the Law of Offense[42] as well as in the jurisdiction of the Municipality Court of Sarajevo, which found that the club is liable under these circumstances.

86. When we consider injuries to spectators, we must also consider the fact of injuries from the spectators to the athletes. This is where the Law on Sport BiH[43] Article 58 stipulates:

> To prevent and combat violence and misconduct of spectators at sports events, Bosnia and Herzegovina and the Entities are required to take the necessary measures under European Convention on the Violence and Misconduct of Spectators at Sports events, especially at football games.
>
> (2) A special law shall determine the manner and measures for preventing and suppressing violence and misconduct of spectators at sports events.

87. The particular Law that was formed, as mentioned above (Article 58.2), highlights tort law and criminal law. As mentioned above, the Law on the Prevention of Violence at Sports Events was formed on entity levels and Districts. In contrast, in the Federation, it is formed on the canton level instead of the entity, and important to mention that not all cantons have adopted such Law. The Law for the entity of RS stipulates the different articles that pertain to the risk of the match and what may be considered punishable under such Law. Considering the above, can we find a club liable for a spectator injury regarding a strike by a ball or sports equipment from the sporting event which caused an injury to the spectator? Courts in BiH have not allowed for recovery of injuries that occur directly from open and obvious rules of the game in which the spectator is evident that such may occur.

II. Criminal Law

88. Wrongful death has also occurred in sporting events and therefore is part of tort law or, under BiH, the Law on Offense, and may be punishable by criminal law. In most essences, we must mention the close relationship and the ability to compare and contrast criminal law and tort law. It is pretty challenging to say which part may apply; it all depends on the circumstances of the case and whether someone may be held responsible due to the death of the person in question that is tied to sporting

41. Latin term meaning the thing speaks for itself. It is a doctrine of law that one is presumed to be negligent if he/she had exclusive control of whatever caused the injury even though there is no specific evidence of an act of negligence, and the accident would not have happened without negligence.
42. *Ibid.*, on 37.
43. *Ibid.*, on 11.

events and sporting organizations. There are no current cases that we may define within the law system of BiH, but it is a question that sporting organizations may face in the future.

89. Another way to look at it, as an example, is the death of a boxer during a competition due to the opponent's injury. The death of the athlete brings up many more questions and ones that have been debated throughout the sporting world. Both athletes were aware of the circumstances before entering the ring and also knew that an injury was something that could occur. When we speak about wrongful death, it is difficult to derive information from the legal system in BiH due to case law that cannot be found. What we can consider is, for example, the club doctor did not take precautions or the athlete competed without the proper medical requirements, and this directly inflicted the cause of the death, as stipulated by the Law on Sport and Law on Offense in BiH, the sporting organization may be held liable for the wrongful death of the athlete.

90. In recent years, international organizations have paid more attention, especially to athletes that have heart conditions and those that receive injuries that cause concussions. The important factor here is to understand the substance of liability and due care during the sporting organization; if the person responsible has taken all necessary precautions, then in most cases, the court would not take into consideration such for negligence or wrongful death. However, for example, a player in a neighbouring country died after hitting a wall too close to the pitch.[44] The family sued the FA because they gave the club and stadium license, not considering the concrete wall that can cause serious injuries during matches and training. As a result, the FA was found guilty of a wrongful death, as they should have taken due care to avoid the possibility of such injuries at the stadium. This can be a circumstance for wrongful death, and due to the lack of case law, we can compare the current structures of the laws and regulations in BiH; the important aspect is whether precautions were taken to avoid such, and there must be an analysis of the facts of the claim.

91. A wrongful death in BiH is challenging to find jurisprudence. Thus, there is a limitation to finding research that can show this aspect. It is imperative to mention that all athletes should go under strict testing before performing, especially if the activity calls for a strain on the body or is considered physical. However, we recently had a case involving FK Sarajevo spectators (away team), Siroki Brijeg spectators (home team), and local police officials. The incident occurred in 2009 when a visiting spectator from the football club FK Sarajevo was killed in front of the stadium of Siroki Brijeg due to a fight between the two ultra-groups.[45] It was a terrible scene but a problematic case for the BiH courts to decide. It was a difficult

44. Staff Reuters, *Croatian Player Dies after Hitting Head on Wall* (last updated Apr. 3, 2008), https://www.reuters.com/article/soccer-europe-croatia-death-idUKL0393548520080403.
45. Balkan Insight, *Sarajevo Fan Died of Gunshot Wound* (updated on Oct. 5, 2009), https://balkaninsight.com/2009/10/05/sarajevo-fan-died-of-gunshot-wound/.

decision because there was no particular case law on the matter; the incident occurred outside of the stadium (who is liable?).

92. Due to high crowds, it was difficult to assess who started the riot and what occurred, besides the fact that a gunshot killed the spectator. The recent decision found that the away spectators caught were charged with tort law and financially liable for their participation in the riot. Unfortunately, due to a lack of clear evidence, the case was dropped against the officer, who was considered the shooter and would have been held criminally responsible for the spectator's death. The fact that the police officer confessed to firing his gun, he could have been held liable due to negligence or criminally prosecuted, which resulted in the death of the spectator. The organizer of the match was difficult to hold liable because the terrible event occurred in front of the stadium instead of the stadium. This case may be considered a stepping-stone for understanding the criminal or civil level of responsibility of all involved during the sporting event or in any particular organization.

III. Public Health and Safety

93. The subject of public health and safety falls within the rights of the entities and Brcko District, like many of the laws and regulations previously stated. However, the Constitution of BiH gives reference in the following Article II (1),[46] which provides that *"BiH and both Entities shall ensure the highest level of internationally recognized human rights and fundamental freedoms."* The Constitution guards the rights of all individuals, but the fact of public health and safety (as mentioned previously) is something that is more so regulated by the entities and Brcko District. Within the FBiH, this particular regulation is again broken down, and the burden lies on the Cantons to implement the necessary regulations and obligations to comply and attend to the public health and safety of person(s).

94. On the entity level of Republika Srpska, the healthcare and thus health and safety is centralized throughout the entity and unlike the FBiH entity, it is less complicated considering the centralized factor. The complications arise when we look at the FBiH with regard to the ability to receive due care for particular health needs. For example, if a person is to be treated in a hospital and has medical coverage, he or she must do so at the Canton in which they are legally registered. This can be seen in the sporting world as well; numerous players have had to list their legal address in the area in which they are playing, to be able to receive the adequate healthcare needed. This allows for the person not having to travel to the Canton in which he or she is registered to be able to wait for healthcare. More often is has been a case in which the legal registered address is shifted to the place of employment to simplify this process. In Brcko District, healthcare and safety are covered for the full territory of the District itself.

46. *Ibid.*, on 23.

95. The lack of a centralized healthcare system on the territory of BiH creates complications, especially for those that tend to move often, and therefore have to shift their legal residence according. To be able to have a clear system put in place for all individuals of BiH, it should not matter where you are treated in BiH, just as long as you have the healthcare covered with regard to the need by the government regulations.

96. Those that are unemployed and of a certain age (not dependent on legal guardians) do not have the necessary health insurance unless they are registered through the local agency for unemployment and an unemployed person, then they might have health insurance. Those that are not registered and of the minority group of the Roma population do not have the health insurance necessary. The complication with the Roma population is the lack of documentation or lack of employment experience, leaving them to have to pay for any medical treatment, as they do not have the insurance needed from the government.

97. With regard to sports, it is another factor we must take into consideration with regard to the type of agreement between the athlete and the sports organization. Technically, only those under an employment contract will have the necessary contributions paid to be able to obtain health insurance. Now, this may present a complication to those athletes competing in clubs or sports that do not have the necessary funds to pay the monthly salary plus tax and contributions (approx. 70%), leaving the athletes without the same treatment as those under an employment contract. To be able to provide security for such athletes, it would be important that all those that are involved in sports have a certain way to provide those without health insurance some type of protection.

98. As stipulated in the Law on Sport BiH,[47] Articles 47 and 48 stipulate the rights for medical and state the following:

> Article 47 (Mandatory health care) (1) Health care is mandatory for all participants in sports. (2) Only a person can participate in sports competitions for whom general and special health fitness has been determined, which is determined by an authorized doctor specializing in sports medicine.
>
> "Article 48 (Conditions for conducting health examinations) The conditions for conducting health examinations of athletes, as well as the way of keeping records and medical documentation of athletes, are prescribed by the entity minister responsible for health, with the opinion of the entity ministry responsible for sports, in accordance with the regulations of international sports federations."

The Federations or Associations, in particular, sports have strict regulations with regard to those competing in sports with regard to health and safety for such. It has been considered the numerous aspects of medical emergencies during sports or health complications; this is why it is imperative to have at least an annual medical

47. *Ibid.*, on 11.

confirmation by the health provider for a person to be able to compete in a sport. This particular law impacts all persons and athletes and therefore extends especially to youth programs.

§5. Relationships Between Ordinary Justice and Sports Justice

99. As stated in an article by Sigmund Lolland, "an attempt is made to articulate what is seen as a 'thin' interpretation of justice in sport and how this is understood in terms of 'thick' interpretations in various sociocultural settings. In this way, it is argued, sport can be better understood as a dynamic social practice."[48] When considering justice in sports, we may look at this in various ways, but in most essences, as mentioned above, it can as well be categorized as a "dynamic social practice." With regard to justice in legal remedies in BiH, it is less common to take the case with regard to sports to ordinary courts in BiH than to specialized legal systems dedicated to sports, such as the CAS or the Disciplinary Committee of the Sports Association. However, there has been significant development if we consider using CAS or justice through particular sports organizations.

100. The implementation of the disciplinary proceedings according to the Sports Federations or Association has given ease to the ordinary justice systems, allowing for the sports federations to be able to decide upon disciplinary proceedings of particular claims. As stipulated within the Statutes of the National FA, the FA has the ability to decide on particular claims within the scope of the Rulebooks adopted by such. The use of the sports disciplinary proceeding allows for certain claims to be decided on a speedy matter and in line with the sports regulations set by the federation. This is a tool used by the sports industry and for the domestic claims that can be ruled upon. When considering the claims with international dimension, the international sporting Federations have adopted procedures to allow for claims to be decided upon within their procedures in place.

101. The ordinary national courts or sports association's disciplinary body tends to make the decisions unless an International Player (Athlete) is involved (as mentioned above), in which a lot of the cases are submitted to FIFA or CAS. For example, in consideration for contractual relationships, financial and other matters that are not usually in connection to the rules of the game may be considered through ordinary courts or by the sports association. This can be brought in front of the relevant sports Federations or Associations, but it is difficult to enforce such decisions other than using the possibility of suspending clubs, banning them from the competition, etc.; this all takes time and, as mentioned, may be difficult to enforce. Therefore, some that are involved in sports claims on a domestic level submit such through the ordinary courts of the respective jurisdiction of the club due to enforcement, especially when the claim brings light to a situation that is not inline between the sports federation and ordinary laws. An example in football, with regard to rules of the game in which a player complains due to yellow cards, a club

48. Sigmund Loland, *Justice in Sport: An Ideal and It's Interpretations*, pp. 78–95 (2007).

complains about fines, and similar cases with regard to the game and not for other factors will most likely be taken into consideration by the FA of BiH.

102. The relationship between the ordinary and sports justice is yet to have a collaborative structure. An example may be seen with the regulations of the FA of BiH, where the player has an employment contract with the club till June 30, but the last match of the season is, let us say, on May 20; the club may consider that the contract expired the first day after the last match of the season. Therefore, the contract by the regulations of the FA is expired on May 21. Regarding the employment contract and ordinary justice, the club would be responsible for paying the player till the end of the contract, June 30. If the player were to seek remuneration for the rest of the contract through the ordinary courts, the club would be responsible, even though the regulations of the FA stipulate differently.

Part II. Private Sports Organizations and Their Regulations

103. The private organizations or when considering the way that the Law on Sports BiH[49] dictates the structure of the different sports stakeholders involved, we can consider Article 16 which states the following:

> Legal entities in the field of sports in the sense of this Law are:
>
> (a) Sports club (amateur and professional).
> (b) Sports club.
> (c) Sports association in a specific sport.
> (d) Sports club of persons with disabilities (amateur and professional).
> (e) Sports association of persons with disabilities.
> (f) Sports association of disabled persons in a certain sport.
> (g) Olympic Committee of Bosnia and Herzegovina.
> (h) Paralympic Committee of Bosnia and Herzegovina.
> (i) Institutions and institutions in the field of sports.

The article defines the way that the law stipulates which body may be considered a legal entity with regard to the laws set forth. The sports stakeholders are set up in a similar way as an association and together follow the procedural laws that are in connection to national, entity, canton and each body shall have internal rulebooks and regulations. Also, stated in Article 31[50] of the Law on Sport with regard to sports organizations define the following:

> Legal entities—sports associations are founded and organized freely and are independent in exercising their rights and obligations, in accordance with this Law, the entity's sports laws, The Law on Associations and Foundations of Bosnia and Herzegovina and the Law on Associations and Foundations of the entity.

49. *Ibid.*, at 11.
50. *Ibid.*

§1. NATIONAL OLYMPIC COMMITTEE

104. The BiH Olympic Committee (OCBiH) is a non-governmental sports association that performs activities following the provisions of the Olympic Charter, the IOC Code of Ethics, the Olympic Movement Anti-Doping Code, the Lausanne Joint Declaration, the Law on Associations and Foundations of BiH and this Law (Articles 24–27 of the Law on Sport of BiH).[51] The Olympic Committee has worked closely with the sports Associations or Federations in the development of sports throughout the country and with the Sporting Sector of the Ministry of Civil Affairs.

105. After its establishment and after the international recognition, OCBiH was registered on December 8, 2002, into the Ministry of Justice's registry as the primary sports organization, in which national sports federations are joined. With the registration and the signing of the Lausanne Declaration on Doping in Sport on June 28, 1999, OCBiH was constituted as a Paramount sports body in BiH.[52]

106. Lausanne Statute, the Law on Associations and Foundations of BiH, and the Law on Sports of BiH have all defined the formation of the Olympic Committee and the recognition of such. As for sports associations, as stated above, clubs and other associations are organized following the Law of Associations and Foundations at the State, Federal, and Canton levels. Therefore, the way the organizational aspect of the OCBIH has been established in a similar manner to the sports clubs and other sports stakeholders within the country.

107. Currently, within the OCBiH, thirty different federations and sports are considered competing Olympic Sports under the umbrella of the OCBiH, and there are currently five non-competing Olympic sports under the same. BiH has established the foundations for competing and non-competing sports and developed the structure to recognize such accordingly. The sports that are currently part of the membership of OCBiH are the following: Athletics, Badminton, Basketball, Bobsleigh, Cycling, Equestrian, Football, Golf, Gymnastics, Handball, Hockey, Judo, Kayak, Luge, Rowing, Rugby, Shooting, Skating, Skeleton, Ski, Swimming, Tennis Table, Taekwondo, Tennis, Triathlon, Volleyball, Water polo, Weightlifting and Wrestling. The list of the sports are the ones with regard to Olympic competing sports, and there are a few others represented within OCBiH but are non-competing sports. The non-competing sports as part of OCBiH are the following: Air sport, Bocce, Chess, Diving, Motorcycle, Special Olympics and Fishing. These are the sports that are all considered part of the membership and have a separate organized Association, Federation, or Union.

108. Most may recall the Winter Olympics held in Sarajevo in the era of 1984 with the use of the rich mountains for the extraordinary event that was to be remembered as the Winter Olympics of Yugoslavia. After the split of Yugoslavia, BiH had its status with the adaptation of the OCBiH. Therefore, making its new path in the

51. *See* National Olympic Comittee of BiH, http://www.okbih.ba/new/lista.php?id=16.
52. *Ibid.*

embark of the Olympic footsteps. First and foremost, holding the wonderful event of the European Youth Olympic Festival (EYOF) in 2019 showed that the country is set to make its path after the split of Yugoslavia. This was an event to remember, as the city with the East Sarajevo (RS) and Sarajevo (FBiH) held an event in collaboration, not looking at whether it was one entity or another, but rather showing that the most important factor is the joining of the city and the entities to respect the honor of Olympics and sport within the country.

109. Regarding the statutes, regulations, and laws within the OCBiH, the executive committee has the power to adopt such, with the approval of the Olympic Committee at the General Assembly.[53] Such recognition gives an organized approach to the laws and regulations regarding the OCBiH. Also, the OCBiH has organized Independent Bodies within the system, which make up the following:

- Supervisory Board of OK BiH.
- Supervision of OK BiH activity.
- Verification of legality in work and material and financial operations in the OK BiH.
- Supervision the execution of decisions and conclusions of the General Assembly and the Executive Committee of OK BiH.
- Verification of compliance with established norms and acts of OK BiH.
- Court of Honor and Sports Arbitration.
- OK, BiH Anti-Doping Control Commission.

110. The Supervisory Board of OK BiH has the jurisdiction regarding the supervision of the activity completed by the OK BiH, verification of legality in the material, work, and financial operations of OK BiH, supervision of the execution of decisions, general Assembly and Executive committee of OK BiH execution, and finally verification of compliance with established norms and acts that are part of OK BiH.

111. Court of Honor and Sports Arbitration is formed due to the following tasks and obligations: to give legal opinions in the domain of the court, resolve disputes with regard to violation of the Statute, the Olympic Charter by an individual, in cases of violation of the dignity of OK BiH by the misconduct of a member of the General Assembly, the Presidency, the Executive Committee or any professional person that works in the OK BiH, and in cases that have a conflict of interest for OK BiH.

112. OK BiH Anti-Doping Control Commission—The commission is formed to control the anti-doping of all athletes and sports that are primarily part of OKBiH—allowing for a unified system in regard to the fight against Anti-Doping.

53. *Ibid.*, at 47.

§2. MAJOR NATIONAL FEDERATIONS

113. Sports Associations or Federations follow the Law on Sport of BiH. Article 22 of the Law on Sport BiH states, "Sports federations are organized at the level of BiH and the Entities, depending on sports development, and at other levels of administrative organization in BiH. Only one may be established at the level of BiH for one sport and sports federation." Thus, the football association/federation of BiH (NS/FS BiH) is organized at the state level and then further down the federations on entity and district levels and finally on the Canton level. Where a dispute occurs on the level of entities or cantons, the decision can be taken to the disciplinary proceedings of the National sports associations/federation and the Council of Ministers BiH. In most essences, all sports associations/federations must abide by the laws of the nation as well as international regulations, such as FIFA or UEFA, in football cases.

Figure 1 Structure of the Football Associations in BiH

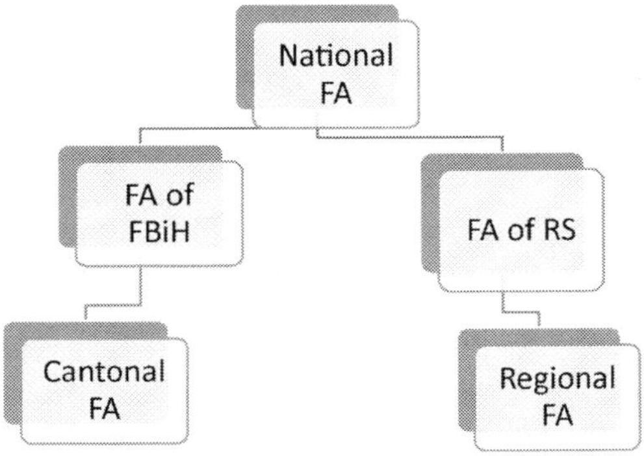

114. The National FA[54] consists of twelve clubs that compete on the national level (Men's BH Telecom Premier League) and in case of disputes between clubs and players registered under the national level, for the issues related to the competition, the National FA has jurisdiction. For all other matters (training compensation, solidarity, transfer fees, etc.), the claimant has to submit the claim to the Regional or Cantonal FA of the respondent (for first instance). The Regional FA[55] consists of seven branches divided geographically throughout the Republik of Srpska, being part of the FA of RS. The Cantonal FA[56] consists of ten branches divided based on cantonal structures within the Federation, being part of FBiH

54. *See* National Football Association of BiH, https://www.nfsbih.ba/.
55. *See also* Republika Srpska Football Association, https://fsrs.org/sr-BA/.
56. *See* The Football Associations of the Federations, https://www.nsfbih.ba/stranica/kantonal niupanijski-nogometni-savezi.

FA.[57] Due to the fact that Brcko District does not have a wide variety of clubs in competition, all the clubs within this entity with regard to football, are part of the FA of RS.[58]

115. At first, this system seems simple and easily understood, but the procedure can have some drawbacks in cases where the dispute is between two clubs or players from different FA's (Regional, Cantonal and their subdivisions). For example, Player A moved from Club B (registered in FBiH-Cantonal FA) to Club C (registered in RS -Regional FA) for a permanent transfer with a fee of EUR 100,000. The Club C failed to pay the transfer fee agreed upon with Club B. Based on jurisdiction, the Regional FA (RS) shall have the right to hear the case and incite procedure upon the request of Club B, since Club C is registered in RS Regional FA. In the case where Club B is not satisfied with the decision, it can appeal the decision further to the National FA.

116. The BiH State Court made an interesting ruling in a case involving officials of the Football Association (NS/FS BiH). The Secretary General of NS/FS BiH Munib Usanovic and the Marketing Secretary Miodrag Kures received a five-year jail sentence for tax evasion and for the abuse of office during the period from 2001 to 2006. After the prison sentence was served, the two were punished with an added five years penalty and forbade them to be able to hold any senior positions in the office of NS/FS BiH. The State Court had the jurisdiction to make the decision due to tax evasion and this particular case could not be ruled by NS/FS BiH proceedings but rather through ordinary courts. The reason behind the ruling above is the fact that the FAs lack the necessary knowledge and legal background to be able to rule against tax evasion. This particular case must be handled by the ordinary courts that have jurisdiction to handle such cases. Within the FA and with regard to cases of this particular nature, it is mostly seen that the case is handled through the ordinary courts. Lack of knowledge and a unified law allows for such decisions to be taken outside of the disciplinary proceedings of the Sports associations and Federations.

117. The clubs are, in essence, part of an Association or Federation on the state, Entity/District, or canton level and therefore have regulations they must abide by. There have been cases in which the national or entity laws only partially follow specific regulations of the sports federation. Therefore, it is one of the most common difficulties. This is where the Law on Sport BiH must have the full right to the jurisdiction of sports associations/federations, clubs, and athletes. The jurisdiction of the sports associations/federations are the following according to Law on Sport BiH Article 23:[59]

(1) Organizing and conducting the competition system.

57. *Ibid.*
58. *Ibid.*, at 50.
59. *Ibid.*, at 11.

(2) Representing the particular sport in international sports organizations, Preparation and appearance of national teams at official international competitions.
(3) Establishing a development program following the strategy.
(4) Cooperation with the competent sports authorities and other bodies of BiH.

In cases with no entity or canton-level sports association, the national-level sports association shall have jurisdiction, with approval from the Ministry of Civil Affairs of BiH.

I. Statutes

118. Considering that football is the primary sport within BiH, we will look at the Statutes of the N/FSBiH (Football Association of BiH). The Statutes align with BiH's national laws regarding registering such on a national level. To understand the organization of the National FA, we must look at Article 9 of the Statutes of the FA,[60] which states that the following shall be the members of the Association:

> NS/FS BIH currently consists of the following two associations:
>
> (1) Football Association of the Federation of Bosnia and Herzegovina (NS FBiH), which consists of ten (10) cantonal/county football associations.
> (2) Football Association of Republika Srpska (FS RS) comprises seven (7) regional football associations:
>   (a) The territorial base of those two associations corresponds to the entities as defined by the Constitution of Bosnia and Herzegovina.
>   (b) Members of NS/FS BIH can be club associations and professional associations (coaches, referees, etc.) if they meet the conditions prescribed by this Statute and if they are subordinate to the NS/FS BiH and acknowledge them.

119. The National FA within the Statutes of such stipulates the rights of all members or stakeholders involved or part of the membership of the National FA. The jurisdiction is stipulated within and shared within the members that are mentioned in the previous paragraph. Also, the statutes define the rights to be able to hear claims on behalf of the procedures set out by the National FA and that if a particular claim goes against the laws of the ordinary courts, a person may as well submit such to the ordinary courts.

120. While looking at the Basketball Association of BiH, there are not as many members of the National Association, and are only the following: Herceg-Bosna Basketball Association, Republika Srpska Basketball Association, Basketball Association Zenica, Sarajevo Canton Basketball Association, Tuzla Regional Basketball Association. Although there is a difference compared to the FA, the essential factor

60. *Ibid.*, at 50.

is that the National Associations/Federations allow for members depending on the level throughout the country. Therefore, the organizational aspect is similar but needs to be improved in the number of members considered part of the National Association/Federation.

II. Main Regulations

121. With regard to regulations, let us look at the FA again in our example of the different regulations that are implemented within the Association/Federation. Without going too broad, the central aspect of the regulations starts with the Statutes, Rulebook of the administrative bodies in the FA, Disciplinary Rulebook, Rulebook of the Registration of Players and Clubs and Status and Transfer of Players, and Rulebook of Play, etc., the regulations within the scope of the FA or Federation allow for better organization between all stakeholders involved within the football industry. An essential factor to consider is that the Association members from other jurisdictions have other regulations but must be in line with the national Association.

122. Considering that the National FA can hear particular claims, it is essential to mention that particular cases may be decided by entity level or canton, depending on the matter. Although a specific claim may entail a club that competes at a national level, the administrative procedure usually starts from the entity level. To give an example, Article 116.3 of the Rulebook on the registration of Players and Clubs and the Status and Transfer of Players[61] stipulates the following:

> for professional players, as well as for amateur players for registration disputes as the second instance authority is the competent commission for the status and transfer of entity players, and if it is about disputed relationship regarding the registration of clubs from different entities as a second-level authority is competent Committee for the status and transfer of NS/FS BiH players.

This particular Article stipulates the ability of the Entity level FA to be part of decisions for particular disputes and when it would be considered on the National level. Therefore, the members of the National Association have jurisdiction over particular matters and entities that deal with situations where the club and athletes are registered in that particular entity. This allows for claims to be quickly submitted and decided upon without waiting for such from the National level. This is just one of the articles that define the jurisdiction, and within the Rulebook, there are other instances of such separation of jurisdiction.

---

61. *Rulebook on the Registration of Players and Clubs and Status and Transfer of Players,* (last updated in 2021), https://www.nfsbih.ba/images/2021-D/Dokumenti_2021/Pravilnik_o_registracijama_klubova_i_igrača_i_statusu_i_transferu_igrača_2021_1._KONAČNI_PRINT_WEB.pdf.

Part III. Sport and Employment

Introduction

Figure 2 Employment Law Structures of BiH[62]

BiH State Level

65 MOR Convention and a number of international treaties (acts The UN and other specialized international organizations).

• Law on Work in the Institutions of BiH ("Official Gazette of BiH" No 26/04, 7/05, 48/05, 60/10 and 32/13),

• Law on strike of employees in the institutions of Bosnia and Herzegovina (Official Gazette of BiH No. 41/16)

• Law on Civil Service in the Institutions of BiH ("Official Gazette of BiH", No.12 / 02, 19 / 02,8 / 03, 35/03, 4/04, 17/04, 26/04, 37 / 04,48 / 05, 2/06, 32/07, 43/09, 08/10 and 40/12)

Brcko District	Republika Srpska (RS)	Federation (FBiH)
Labor Law ("Official Gazette of the Brcko District" No.19 / 06-consolidated text, 19/07, 25/08, 20/13, 31/14 and 1/15), • Law on Strike ("Official Gazette of the Brcko District" No. 3/06) • Law on Safety and Health Protection of Workers (»Official Gazette Brcko District of BiH »no. 20/13) • Law on Civil Service in Brcko District Public Administration Bodies ("Official Gazette of the BDBiH" No. 9/14, 37/15, 48/16 and 9/17) • Law on Officials and Employees of the Judiciary of the BDBiH ("Sl.glasnik BDBiH "no. 36/07, 2/08 and 6/13) • Employment and unemployment ("Official Gazette of the BDBiH" No.33 / 04, 19/07 and 25/08); • Law on Employment of Foreigners in the Brcko District of BiH ("BDBiH Official Gazette" Nos. 15/09, 19/09 and 20/10)	Labor Law ("Official Gazette of the RS" No. 1/16, 66/18); • Law on Occupational Safety ("Official Gazette of the RS" 1/08 and 13/10) • Law on Workers' Advice ("Official Gazette of the RS" No 26/01); • Law on employment mediation and unemployment rights ("Official Gazette of RS" Nos. 30/10 and 102/12); • Law on Employment of Foreign Nationals and Stateless Persons («Official Gazette RS »No. 24/09 and 117/11); • Law on Civil Servants ("Official Gazette of the RS" No 118/08, 117/11, 37/12, 57/16) • Law on civil servants and employees in the bodies of the local unit self-government (" RS Official Gazette ", No. 97/16) • Law on Professional Rehabilitation and Employment of Disabled Persons («Official Gazette RS »No.37 / 12 and 82/15); • Law on Strike ("Official Gazette of RS" No. 111/08);	Labor Law (FBiH Official Gazette 26/16), • Law on Strike (FBiH Official Gazette 14/00), • Law on Employment of Foreigners (FBiH Official Gazette 111/12), • Law on the Employee Council (Official Gazette of BiH No. 39/04), • Law on Occupational Safety (Official Gazette of SR BiH No. 22/90 is in procedure passing a new law), • Law on Civil Service in the FBiH ("Official Gazette FBiH "No.29 / 03.23 / 04.39 / 04.54 / 04.67 / 05, 8/06, 4/12), • Law on State Employees in the Civil Service FBiH ("FBiH Official Gazette" No. 49/05).

62. Mehmed, Hadzic, *Izvori Radnog Prava* [Sources of Employment Law] (publsihed 2018).

123. As can be seen from the illustration above, not all entities have the same laws as one another and that may be defined differently. Also, it is important to keep in consideration that the federation has ten Cantons within the entity and therefore the employment law stretches out further in detail. This can be confusing as it is not as unified throughout the country, therefore leaving room for clarification of the jurisdiction on a claim-to-claim basis.

124. Considering that an Athlete has a specific time limit in his career and that the working hours of an athlete vary and cannot compare that to most other workers (or that as defined by Employment Law, such as someone selling coffee at a coffee shop), then we can conclude that numerous issues can be mentioned. A few key aspects that can be considered complications when looking at employment in sports in BiH can be the following:

- Working hours of athletes compared to others.
- Retirement age.
- Laws and regulations that contradict each other compared to sports and national laws.
- Employment law and contracts on employment are strict and thus challenging to implement in sports.

125. These are just a few general issues we may find when discussing sports and employment law. Currently, the laws stipulate that an athlete has the same rights as any other person and that such laws shall apply, therefore due to the lack of further in-depth Sports Laws in BiH, sports organizations are left to apply employment law that is in definite on the rights and what shall stipulate as an employment. In practice, there are frequent cases where minors conclude sponsorship and engagement contracts with the clubs where they train, whereby the clubs are obliged to provide minor players with certain benefits such as, for example:

- Free training.
- Equipment for training.
- Nutrition and nutritional supplements.
- Certain amount of monthly stipend, along with others.

In practice, it is common for clubs to stipulate certain obligations in this type of contract in order to "secure" the investment in the same way that the provisions of the same stipulate obligations:

(i) That the minor player must, after coming of age, conclude a professional contract with the club, which will be determined by the club with which he has concluded a contract.
(ii) That he may not terminate the contract, and if he does so, he is obliged to:
   - Return double the amount of the invested investment to the club with which the contract has been concluded.
   - Pay the contractual penalty.

126. It is important to emphasize that the local courts, in principle, accept the method mentioned above of "insurance" as a legal one. Although, as a rule, they accept lawsuits and order the payment, i.e., the return of double the amount of the invested funds, while depending on how the provisions of the contract are drafted, it is questionable whether it is possible to cumulate the obligation to return double the amount invested and the contractual penalty, which certainly exists as a separate legal institution of the law of obligations. For now, there still needs to be an appropriate practice of local courts that would fully resolve this dilemma.

127. Following the above, the retirement age must be considered. Athletes retire relatively early in their careers. Therefore, their contributions to social security are based on the fact that they are an employee like any other employee in a company or organization. This also ties a lot into the taxation and contributions of the employment contract. To achieve total contributions regarding pension, the athlete must be signed to 8 hours a day, and not for the period they spend working, which can be from 2–6 hours per day. Suppose the athlete is signed up for fewer working hours. In that case, you have a question of whether they are full-time or part-time employees, and to make it even more complicated, if they are part-time, how do we consider the preparation period where most sports organizations spend 7–15 days away from home and with the sports organization? Therefore, the athlete has more than 8 hours a day at work, considering that he is in the preparations away from home and work. This can be seen as a 24-hour period, considering their limitations to being home.

128. Then, the national associations of the sporting organizations (e.g., FAs) have regulations, which sometimes are not in conjunction with the national laws (as mentioned previously). This is where there are the most complications as to which law shall prevail and whether the national associations can adapt their laws to the national laws, considering the international federations (such as UEFA/FIFA), which may impose for the national associations to adapt their regulations within the sporting association of the country belonging to the international federation.

129. Finally, contracts are considered employee contracts; the professional playing contract is only considered a standard employment contract. This is a strict rule; therefore, we need more clarification regarding part-time contracts, as they are not regarded to the full extent of an employment contract, especially in the circumstances of contributions.

§1. Sources of Employment Law

I. Ordinary Law

130. The sources of employment law in BiH can be derived from several different acts, such as the Employment Law of FBiH 26/16,[63] the Employment Law of

63. *See* Employment Law in FBiH, (*"Official Gazzete"* No. 26/16).

RS,[64] the Employment law of Brcko District,[65] and regulations from sporting associations.[66] The above concerns national laws and does not consider the international dimension of laws or regulations that apply to athletes and their employment status under the national associations and sporting organizations. Therefore, when considering national laws, the sporting organization must follow as stated above and implement the laws starting from the National level, Entity/District, and finally, the sporting associations. Deriving from the above information, the sporting associations can only implement contracts that align with the country's laws, or at least they are only legally considered applicable if they are in line with the ordinary laws on employment. Therefore, the country's ordinary laws are the highest power above that of sporting associations. Therefore, to understand the complex employment law system within BiH, it is best to define the different laws that are split from country to entity.

131. As seen from the illustration above, not all entities have the same laws as one another, and they may be defined differently. It is also essential to consider that the federation has ten Cantons within the entity; therefore, the employment law stretches further in detail. This can be confusing as it needs to be more unified throughout the country, leaving room for clarification of the jurisdiction on a claim-to-claim basis.

132. Considering the numerous entities within BiH and that in the case of national sources of employment law, it would be challenging to analyze all, but for the circumstance of understanding employment law within the country, the following shall be focused on the Federation Entity. Further, we will analyze circumstances with direct differences between the entities. In the FBiH and the Employment Law of FBiH 26/16, Article 20[67] states that:

(1) With the person(s) under age 15, it is illegal to conclude an employment contract, and such shall be seen as not binding.
(2) With the person(s) between the ages of 15 and 18 (in other words: Minors), the law allows for the minors to enter into a contract or be employed solely if the legal guardian has signed the contract and thus given permission and only after an official medical institute or doctor has made a medical check and signed off that the minor can be employed and is healthy.

133. Article 20 is essential when considering sports in BiH because, in many cases, athletes are signed relatively young for the sporting organization. A minor in BiH is considered to be anyone under the age of 18. The complications of signing minors have been battled throughout European sports organizations, as many clubs

64. (Employment Law in RS, "Official Gazzet of RS," Nos. 1/2016, 66/2018, 91/2021—Decision US i 119/2021).
65. (Employment Law of Brcko District, "Official Gazzet Brčko distrikta BiH," Nos. 34/2019, 2/2021, 6/2021 and 15/2022).
66. The Football Association of BiH—this is a unified association for the respect of the top of the associations pyramid (furthermore, we must consider Entity Associations, and Canton).
67. *Supra* at 58.

are bound to sign youth to their sports organization. However, many countries have strict rules for signing minors to employment law and the age at which they may be executed. For example, in football, if the player is signed after age 18, the club risks losing him after he is no longer a minor or to other clubs in the country before 18. This is where we must consider the age, the law that stipulates such, and national federations that engage their regulations regarding minors. In addition, sporting associations must consider international regulations and ordinary local laws regarding the employment of minors.

134. Furthermore, not considering the laws and regulations mentioned above, most all-sporting organizations have internal rulebooks that stipulate and define the obligations and rules of employees and employers. The internal rulebook shall not go against national regulations and laws but rather simplify certain aspects, such as what constitutes wrongdoing by the employee and what relief the employee or employer has. In most instances, it is requested that if the sports organization has more than twenty employees, they have an internal rulebook. This can also be considered a company or club collective agreement part of the athlete's contract. Once the athlete decides to sign the contract, they may have an article stating that the employee or athlete must consider the company's or club's rulebook. It has been shown that there have been numerous examples in which such is stated in the rulebook, but the employee/athlete has never seen such or is not aware. Clubs and sporting organizations in BiH have started implementing that all employees sign that they have received the internal rulebook mentioned within the contract. This leaves less room for such to be questioned if brought about in a claim.

135. Employment relationship is mentioned within the Law on Sport BiH[68] in Article 35 which states the following:

(1) Legal entities can establish a working relationship with athletes, professional workers, professional and administrative staff.
(2) Employment in sports organizations, as legal entities registered at the level of BiH, is governed by an employment contract in accordance with the Labor Law institutions of BiH ("Official Gazette of Bosnia and Herzegovina," Nos. 26/04, 7/05 and 48/05).
(3) The employee has all the rights and obligations from the employment relationship established by the Law from paragraph (2) hereof member, the collective agreement and this Law.
(4) Employment in sports associations as legal entities at the entity level and other levels of administrative organization are regulated by the employment contract in accordance with corresponding regulations at that level.

Employment and Law on Sport BiH show that the status of an athlete or the contractual relationship ties in with the ordinary laws and such must be respected no matter the sector that is involved.

---

68. *Ibid.*, at 11.

II. Collective Bargaining Agreements

136. Collective Bargaining Agreements (CBA) and the connection to sports have been seen through different sports in the contract. It is essential to understand that most of the time, the CBA is not signed between the club and the representative of the CBA but rather that the CBA or Union works independently and seeks membership in the respective National or entity Association. In football, a Union for footballers was formed in connection with FIFPRO (international level), but such a Union has no signed agreements with particular clubs. The football union works with players to assist their needs toward their employer or even represent them in claims.

137. The Union is a membership basis association that works solely on the membership fees paid by the players for the player to seek their rights in front of the club or association. In minimal instances, the players seek a collective right to be handled as a group. Therefore, in most instances, the Union assists the players moving forward.

138. The sports associations allow the unions to become national association members. However, in this instance, the football union is separate from the clubs and the FA. This has been an improvement in the assistance of players to seek relief without always having to acquire the services of a lawyer. As mentioned previously, the core factor of the Union's functioning is to seek and assist with players' rights.

§2. Status of Players

139. BiH athletes can practice sports as a professional or amateurs. However, when it comes to a professional athlete, it is a classic employment relationship whereby the athlete concludes an employment contract or, in other words, a professional contract, and in that case, the athlete has all the rights guaranteed by the Labor Law; he/she is entitled to a salary for the work completed and the right to payment of contributions, pension, health insurance, unemployment insurance, food consumption, recourse, and additionally such. The status of players is defined by the Law on Sport and Regulations within the respective sports stakeholders.

140. Prior to defining the status of a player, it is important to reiterate the fact that an athlete or player is first recognized as an individual and the rights of the person are at the forefront prior to what the status may be as a player. Currently, even though BiH has the status of professionals and amateurs, in some of the collective sports, the professional status is not as predominate. The reason that some of the collective or team sports do not have a "professional team or players" is the fact that a professional must have an employment contract (professional contract) with the sports clubs. In retrospect to the above, some of the clubs in particular sports do not have the financial availability to pay for the salaries, contributions, and taxes, therefore, reverting to amateur contracts to reduce the burden. This is why the status of players may be defined and regulated to an extensive level; the fact remains that the status is only such if the player is registered and has a contract that reflects such.

141. There have been cases in which a player was registered with the relevant sports federation or association as an Amateur (to avoid the financial burden of an employment contract, in terms of tax and contribution) but with the financial gain of the player and the status within the team, the player was considered a professional. This has also been important with regard to the recognition of training compensation[69] (football), where the player's status was only registered as an amateur to avoid the payment to a former potential club, but such status was proven through the facts of the financial and status of the player.

142. In the case of an amateur athlete, the employment contract is not concluded. However, an "amateur contract"[70] which is considered an agreement without pay or just for the expenses of playing has a legal basis in the Law on Obligations, and the specificity of the amateur contract is that the employer does not pay contributions for pension, health insurance, unemployment insurance, additionally such. In BiH, many athletes have amateur contracts and can only move freely between clubs during the season once an official transfer window is opened. Therefore, a football player playing for a club with an amateur contract must wait for the transfer window, although the contract is not as binding as the employment contract.

143. When considering the international source of the legal status of players, it is similar in all instances that the player is differentiated between amateur and professional status. The FIFA RSTP[71] stipulates the differences, and in most instances, the professional football player earns more than the expense he incurs from playing football. However, the amateur may earn some salary, but it is less than the expenses he incurs from football. This has been adopted by the regulations of the NS/FS BiH.

144. It must be mentioned that players under 18 (minors) can have a status as a professional within a sport. However, a minor under the age of 15[72] is not able to conclude an employment contract; within the age of 15 and above, the minor may sign a contract, but it is only valid if the legal guardian signs together with the

69. Training compensation with regard to football is the payment for the football education to previous clubs that trained the player from age 12 till 21 and when the player signs the first professional contract from that period until age 23 (can be paid to former clubs). The full explanation may be found in the FIFA Regulations on the Status and Transfer of Players (updated on March 2022).

70. In some countries, the amateur does not even have a contract, because this particular status means that the athlete is not paid for his work but rather could be considered on a basis of a scholarship contract or part time contract. In BiH, all athletes either have a professional contract (employment contract) or amateur contract (scholarship, service or part time contract).

71. *Ibid.*, on 62. *FIFA RSTP* Art. 2 (Scope of Players) details the definition of athletes and how they are to be considered. This is in most cases than interpreted into the national football association, thus assisting when regulating the contracts and employment of players.

72. *Ibid.*, on 58 Art. 20.

minor, giving the legal right for the minor to be employed. Also, within the employment laws, it is stipulated that the minor must go through a particular medical exam to receive the certificate to be competent to work at a particular age. The complication of this law is that athletes who sign a professional contract with a club under 18 cannot attend school full-time. However, instead, they must register school as a part-time activity while having employment/professional contracts. The following paragraphs shall show in detail the differences between the status of an amateur and a professional player.

I. Professionals

145. A Professional Athlete in the context of sports in BiH must have a signed contract of employment with the club that he participates with. In context of a professional when considering football, the N/FSBiH Rulebook on the Registration of Players and Clubs and Status and Transfer of Players,[73] Article 63 states that a football player is considered a professional if he/she is paid more than the expenses for competing in football. Also, the player must have paid contributions by the club, similar to any other employee on an employment contract. Another factor is that at least eleven players within the first team must have a professional contract when the club is competing in the Premier League.

146. The Professional contract of a Football Player must be on a minimum basis of the full season of the BiH Premier League and the maximum that the contract may be signed is for the maximum of five years. For players that are under the age of 18, they may sign a professional contract but with the signing of one of their legal guardians. Within the above regulations, there is a stipulation in which a player may be registered to compete in a different sport (e.g., from Football to Futsal), but only if the initial club in which the player is registered gives approval for the signing of such. There have been a few instances in which football players were able to compete in the eleven aside football and sign with a futsal team, but usually competing during the off-season of the eleven aside.

II. Amateurs

147. Amateur Athletes are considered those that play a certain sport for fun and considering football again, the amateur player may only receive enough funds to cover expenses but anything above this amount will be considered a professional athlete. There have been numerous instances in which a player has signed an amateur contract, but during a dispute, the contract was interpreted as a professional contract.

73. *Ibid.*, on 54.

148. If we look at the N/FSBiH Rulebook mentioned above, the club that signs an agreement with a player as an amateur, then the club must cover the following expenses (Article 59.2):

> The costs that the club is obliged to pay to the amateur player are:
>
> (a) Travel and accommodation costs when the club goes to competitions and preparations.
> (b) Costs of enhanced nutrition.
> (c) Costs of work/sports equipment.
> (d) Travel costs.

The players that are still attending school may have a status as an amateur but the payment of expenses or the scholarship for the player must be in line with the same Regulations and Article 59.3[74] which states:

> If the club and the player agree on the player's scholarship, the costs of the monthly scholarship for players' education can be determined in the maximum amount provided by the entity's positive regulations.

Considering that the players attend school and have the ability to receive a scholarship, they must abide by the decisions for the amount in the entity they are going in school and with the club they are registering with. Therefore, the amount of scholarship is not defined by the National FA but rather by the entity and Ministry of Education for the particular entity.

149. The amateur contract may be signed with a minor from the age of 14 and on a full season but cannot be signed longer than six months during the winter transfer window. The complication that has been seen with regard to amateur status is that clubs are not protected because the amateur agreement is not binding like the employment contract.

§3. Employment Relationship

150. The employment relationship has been mentioned briefly in the previous paragraphs but to continue with regard to the understanding, Article 27 of Law on Sport RS[75] stipulates the relationship between an athlete and a club with the following within the article:

(1) The contract between the athlete and the sports organization is concluded in writing and registered in accordance with the rules of the competent republican sports federation.

74. *Ibid.*, on 54.
75. *Ibid.*, on 31.

(2) The method and necessary elements of the registration of the contract from paragraph 1 of this article shall be determined by the competent national sports association.

(3) All status contractual changes related to termination, term of validity, disciplinary measures suspending the right to perform and assigning the athlete to another sports organization are registered with the competent republican sports association.

(4) The sports organization is obliged to inform the RS sports association about the changes referred to in paragraph 3 of this article within three days from the day of the change or the next day if the change occurred during the transitional and registration period determined by the calendar of the RS sports association.

(5) A dispute under a contract between an athlete and a sports organization due to non-fulfillment of contractual obligations shall be resolved by a sports arbitration decision regarding the athlete's status.

(6) Due to non-fulfillment of contractual obligations, legal proceedings may be initiated before the competent court.

151. The above shows the main items in consideration of the relationship between the club and the athlete with regard to clubs registered in the territory of the RS entity. Considering that FBiH Entity does not have a law on sport on this level, the next step would be the consideration of the cantons and Brcko District. The main aspect of the regulations within the Sports Federations and Law on Sport is that the consideration of Labor Law or Employment Law must have precedence with regard to guarding the relationship. This is important to stipulate, as in certain situations, we have the mention of employment relationships in detail to the law on sport on different levels, but lack of such can be seen in some of the cantons. For example, the Sarajevo Canton and Law on Sport Canton Sarajevo does not give much information or detail as to how work employment is implemented. Therefore, the factor to take into consideration would have to be employment law within the jurisdiction in question.

152. The contradictions between the regulations of the National Associations and those of Labor or Employment Law leave an uncertain situation for stakeholders and athletes. To comprehend the severity of this, the main analysis will be that of the National FA and the differences. The National FA has a standard professional employment contract that must be used by the clubs, and within such, the clubs are allowed to set a maximum duration of five years for a player over the age of 18.

In Article 65.1 states that:

> the minimum duration of the contract is the period from the date of its entry into force until the end of the season, while the maximum duration of the contract is five years.[76]

This particular article is contradictory to the laws on labor (Employment Laws).

76. *Ibid.*, on 54.

The Employment Law of FBiH states under Article 22.3:

> A fixed-term employment contract cannot be concluded for a period longer than three years.[77]

This is one example from the Federation entity but on the RS level, we have a similar situation but even less than in the FBiH. Article 39.2 states that:

> the employer and employee may conclude one or more employment contracts from paragraph 1 of this article for a period that, with or without interruptions, cannot exceed a total of 24 months.[78]

Both the entity level has a regulation that contradicts the Rulebook set out by the National FA.

153. The arise to the contradiction leaves plenty of room for claims to be submitted to the ordinary courts due to the fact that if in the FBiH, the employee has a contract longer than three years, his contract automatically transitions to a contract for indefinite duration. The same application is given within the entity of RS. Clubs have found ways to avoid indefinite contracts but still leave both the club and the player in a vulnerable place. The contract has to cease after three years or in RS two years, and the player cannot be employed for a period that is not less than thirty days (RS) while in the FBiH, it is left for the courts to decide whether the employee has the right for the indefinite period.

154. Brcko District has the same article as that of RS entity for the duration of twenty-four months and may re-engage with the employer after a cease of the initial employment contract for more than fifteen days and only then will this not be considered an indefinite employment contract. In most circumstances, the contradicting regulations have not been part of a claim involving an athlete and a sports organization due to the lack of knowledge of the athlete of the contradicting regulations. It has been more predominant with coaches and staff to use this particular regulation in the midst of having an indefinite contract with the club, leaving clubs with coaches that have been there for more than ten or even twenty years.

155. Players have submitted cases to NS/ FS BiH for resolution of non-payment of salaries. Therefore, the clubs have lost the ability to compete in the premier league of BiH due to league licensing. The club's obligations to their employers are overlooked by the UEFA Licensing and the National club licensing of NS/FS BiH for the premier league (2018).[79] When discussing further the employment contract of players, there have been cases where the regulations of a sports association are contradictory to the Employment Law. For example, Article 76 of the NS/FS BiH

77. *Ibid.*, on 58.
78. *Ibid.*, on 31.
79. *Pravilnik o Licenciranju Klubova za učešće u takmičenju Premijer liga BiH* [Rulebook on Licensing of Clubs for participation in the BiH Premier League competition] (updated on 2018).

RSTP states that if the player's contract expires at either the end of the season or half-season, the contract shall be deemed expired on the day after the last official match before the winter or summer transfer window (previously mentioned). This particular law is against the employment law of BiH or entities because the contract has not fully expired, and the ordinary courts need to recognize the regulation set forth by the NS/FS BiH. This Article has shown the gray area of sports regulations in BiH and the laws that govern employment in BiH.

A similar case occurred in FK Sarajevo; a player sued the club for terminating the contract before expiration, and because the club did not pay a contribution on tax, the player received the full pay and the tax and contributions that were attributed to the dispute. This is only one matter that has occurred in which we can confirm that there is a need for a unified system between the regulations of a sports association and that of ordinary state laws. To move forward, it would be essential to protect the players and the clubs by unifying the regulations and giving light to the fact that there have been numerous disagreements on this matter.

156. The employment relationship, as already mentioned, is similar to any other industry and in line with the laws of the nation, entities, districts and with collaboration with sports stakeholders. To be able to improve the relationship with regard to the employment aspect, it would be important to tailor the contracts in line with the work completed. Therefore, in sports, we would have a simplified situation instead of having to work around the different jurisdictions. The other agreements that have been completed by sports stakeholders (clubs) have been even service agreements, allowing for remuneration but with a lower tax rate.

I. Employment Agreements

157. Employment agreements are an important factor in protecting both the club and the athlete. The employment agreements usually entail the clubs and athletes' obligations, duration, potential bonuses and salary. With regard to Football, any employment agreement, annex, or similar thereof must be verified by the entity FA and the National FA before the player is fully registered and to be able to compete in official matches.

The N/FSBiH supplies the clubs with a draft of the mandatory requirements to be with each player who signs a professional contract with the club. This professional or employment contract may have added other articles or regulations, but the mandatory factor must be the basic aspect of such agreement.

158. As discussed above, the athletes or players must have an employment contract similar to that of any other employee and in the previous paragraphs, there was the mention of the contradictions of the duration of the contract. Another factor which would be important to distinguish but currently not part of the professional contracts is the actual job position of the player signing the agreement. In previous years, it has been a complication with regard to players that have had an employment agreement for the job of "Professional Player" but not defining whether this person is part of the senior team, reserve team or similar thereof. This complication arose due to the fact that some players are sent to train with a smaller group of reserves until medically fit or for reasons that the club may have. With this in mind, this particular situation was used in a few instances to punish players, although it can be debated whether such would be upheld, especially in ordinary courts. To make sure there is no room for clubs to abuse the job title, it would be positive to have a strict job description with regard to the particular team the player is joining or at least have a contract that defines more in detail. For example, an Academy Professional Player may be directed by the club for the senior team.

159. If certain items are not mentioned within the employment agreement, they must be stated within the collective rulebook or agreement of the club, and such shall be supplied to the player or employee at the signing of the agreement or contract. The rulebook may have information on the termination clauses, disciplinary proceedings, duration of vacation and additional items, but all must be in line with the respective laws of the entities and Brcko District.

160. As mentioned previously, the employment agreements have some contradictions according to the National Federations and those of the entity or District. The important factor is that the laws of the particular entity in which the club is registered must abide first and foremost by the entity laws, canton laws or District. Even though there is a contradiction of the regulations, it is important to understand which body of jurisdiction has the final say, and in this instance, the National FA may have said, but the factor is that the legislation or laws adopted by the entity or district have the higher power. Currently, there is no jurisprudence to assist in the understanding of what would occur when the two contradictions implement the employment agreement of the player, although within the regulations, we can assume a conclusion that would be according to the state, entity and district laws.

161. The employment agreements that the athletes sign, in most instances, mention that the National Federation should handle the claims with regard to the agreement, but a separate article within the agreements will usually always stipulate that the laws of employment will prevail in the decision where a particular article may be contradictory. This is important to mention because in instances where employment law prevails and even if the National Federation may have the ability to hear the claim, it shall work in line with the laws of employment of the respective clubs located jurisdiction (entities or district).

162. The working hours within BiH are similar to most countries within the region, at least for full-time adults. The full-time working hours in BiH is forty hours per week, and if the employee is a minor, then the working hours may not surpass thirty-six hours per week. Article 36 of the Employment Law of FBiH and Article 47 of the Employment Law of RS give the regulations with regard to the number of hours to be considered a full-time employee. The complications that we have touched basis on is the fact that athletes or players do not have the same type of work day as in other industries; therefore, their working hours cannot compare and sometimes may be from two hours to twenty-four hours, depending on traveling with team and training or matches.

163. As stated in the employment laws of the entities and Brcko District, it is the obligation of the employer to supervise or take evidence of the working hours of all employees that are employed by the particular company. Therefore, the players would need to stamp in and stamp out or have other ways of evidence taking to confirm the actual hours spent working, and this has been a common debate over the years between sports workers and governmental institutions. The evidence of working hours is not written directly to the corresponding hours spent at the pitch or other sports infrastructure or office. The evidence of the working hours is used for the full calculation of the gross salary of the employee; therefore, without the evidence, the club should not be able to calculate the actual salary of the employees.

164. It was briefly mentioned, but it may be important to reiterate that any benefit that a player receives outside the scope of the salary is taxed as if it were part of the income. This is why clubs have difficulty in incorporating bonuses for matches or offering accommodation paid for by the club. As well, clubs tried offering official club cars for the use of the players, but all of this was an extra benefit for the employee and subject to taxes according to the initial salary of the player. This has given BiH a decrease in attractiveness with regard to the other neighboring countries, considering that in Serbia, bonuses are taxed less than the player's salary. In Croatia, players have been known to open up companies to be able to invoice the club and this has been a practice that was frowned upon by the football community but was to reduce the stress of tax on sports.

165. The employment agreement, once signed by the parties, must be verified by the National Federation to be able to comply with the regulations. Such was mentioned, the verification is an important step, as clubs have been known for using double contracts with two companies or for the lack of complying with the minimum agreement requirements set by the National Federation. This is to make sure that the clubs comply with the regulations and contract details. Recently, a player was left in an unheard-of situation in which he could have submitted a claim, but it was mutually resolved. The player signed a new agreement with the club and terminated the previous agreement. The new agreement was for the duration of six months (minimum contract is for at least a full season), the FA denied the contract, but due to an error, they terminated his previous agreement and the player was left without an active contract due to the error of the club and the FA with regard to the procedure. This is why it is important to have the verification process in place, to avoid potential claims that may arise due to the initial agreement details; of course, in this situation, the FA reacted poorly due to first terminating the contract before actually realizing that the new agreement was null and void.

II. Player's Obligations

166. The Law on Sport BiH in Article 40[80] stipulates the obligations of athletes as according to this law, the following applies:

The athlete is obliged to:

(a) Respect the norms and rules of sports behavior.
(b) Regularly train and participate in competitions.
(c) Respect sports rules, officials and spectators.
(d) Protect the reputation of the sports team and the environment it represents with his behavior.
(e) Cooperate with health services and special bodies that check the use of illicit stimulants.

Similar obligations are given throughout the regulations of different authority bodies and in consideration of the national laws, entities, cantons and federations. The player has decided to participate in a sport and his or her obligations are just as simple as mentioned above. Of course, each sports federation or club may extend the obligations according to their visions and goals, but the core aspect with regard to the law is the above-mentioned Article 40.

167. It has briefly been mentioned with regard to the different obligations of both parties, the employer (Club or Sports Organization) and the employee (Athlete or Player). As stated by the official professional contract by the National FA, the player is obliged to complete the following when with an agreement to the club:[81]

- The player undertakes to play Football/Soccer for the club to the best of his ability, to train and prepare for the club's matches. The player undertakes to use all his sporting abilities, knowledge and skills in favor of the club and to avoid anything in his behavior that could diminish the reputation of the club or negatively affect the club's sports results or other activities and operations of the club.
- The player undertakes to participate in all competitions and training sessions of the club, in all player agreements and other activities related to preparations for matches and competitions, including trips in the country and abroad by means of transport determined by the club.
- By signing this contract, the player transfers to the club the right to use the image and name. This right applies to the use of the player's likeness in all current and future public media and institutions, including multimedia, and in particular, applies to the use of the player's photographs permitted by the club.

The above are just some obligations that a football player may have with the club with regard to a professional contract. The main aspect of the agreement is that the player is to train and play matches and uphold the highest obligations with regard

80. *Ibid.*, on 11.
81. *Ibid.*, on 50.

to that of an athlete. He is not able to gamble or sponsor rival partners without the consent of the club, obliged to show up to training on time or as stipulated by the coaching or administration staff. In some instances, you will see in the contract that the player is obliged to market or be on television for an amount of times per week. These are just standard contracts with regard to the obligations.

III. Player's Rights

168. Law on Sport BiH[82] Article 39.2 dictates the rights of athletes with the following:

(2) In addition to the rights from Article 37 of this Law, the athlete has the right to:
  (a) Be protected from any type of spiritual and physical violence, threats to freedom of human and sports integrity, health and sports dignity.
  (b) Use sports facilities and equipment, services professional work and health care in accordance with the regulations.
  (c) On the basis of freely expressed will, participates in representative selections.

The rights of players or athletes must be defined, and according to the above regulations, such are defined throughout the respective jurisdictions, laws, regulations, and sports stakeholders. The importance of defining a separate right to that of athletes, unlike that of just any employer, is that the risk within certain sports can be higher than working in a different industry. Therefore, the detailed rights give the ability for the athletes to have protection and understanding of what they may expect as their rights.

169. The most important factor to stipulate is that a professional player has the same standard that is given to any employee with regard to the territory in which he is registered to the particular sports organization. Therefore, the player is initially considered an employee and therefore he has the protection of the particular employment law in that entity or District. The next, in regard to those that have a professional status, is stipulated within the agreement above which the player has a right to a day of rest within the week and paid vacation at the end of the season and, in some circumstances, during the half season. The player has the right to seek medical care for injuries, especially those that occur while playing for the club and, therefore, the coverage must be given.

170. Each athlete or player has the right to receive adequate sports equipment from the club to be able to train or play matches. The same right is stipulated in the contract or the club's internal rulebooks (in most cases, it is mentioned in both). The initial rights of each player is to be able to participate in training and matches; during this time, the player must receive equal treatment unless defined differently by

82. *Ibid.*, on 11.

the rulebook. For example, if the player is returning to play from an injury, he may need assisted training with individual work prior to teamwork, and in this instance, the training will be a bit different than that of the rest of the team.

171. Important to again stipulate that the player's rights are that of any individual, especially according to ordinary laws. The player may not be discriminated against for any particular reason, or taken away the ability for training and competition when there is not a reason for doing so.

IV. Clubs Obligations

172. The club is obliged to support the players with regard to the above obligations and rights. As stated within the previous paragraphs, the club is obliged to provide each player with equipment, sports appeal for training, transportation to and from matches, medical staff, and the ability to participate in training and matches. The previous paragraph details more of the supplied obligations of the club when in regard to sports. If we look from the perspective of the contract, the club is obliged to pay the gross salary of each and every player, which means the net amount plus taxes and contributions mentioned in the agreement.[83] Also, the clubs must ensure that each player (no matter the status) has the ability to receive treatment for any injury or medical need arising from the sport.

173. The Law on Sport BiH with regard to legal entities and as mentioned in Article 31 states that "legal entities are founded and organized freely and are independent in exercising their rights and obligations, in accordance with this Law, the entity's sports laws, The Law on Associations and Foundations of Bosnia and Herzegovina and the Law on Associations and entity foundations." The particular law defines the club's obligation in regard to adapting within the laws that dictate sports and stakeholders. The difficulty is that there are still contradicting matters between the federation regulations and those within the laws of the country (as an example: Employment Law). The clubs are obliged to be registered as a legal entity within the respective jurisdiction and, according to the Law on Sport BiH, to be able to commence the work as a stakeholder or club.

174. After considering the Law on Sport BiH, another factor to consider is what may be defined by the entity, district or cantons. In Article 45[84] of the Law on Sport RS entity, the following are the obligations to be able to be considered a club:

(1) A sports organization can perform sports activities if, in addition to the conditions prescribed by the sports rules, it also must have:
   (1) Athletes who are members or engaged under a contract.
   (2) Engaged sports experts depending on the type of activity.
   (3) Adequate space provided, i.e., sports facilities and sports equipment.

83. *Ibid.*, on 50.
84. *Ibid.*, on 31.

(4) Appropriate internal organization.

(2) The word "club" can only be used in the name of a sports organization that participates in competitions within the competent sports federation.

(3) If the sports organization is not a member of the RS sports federation, the conditions from paragraph 1 of this article are determined according to the sports rules of the RS sports federation.

(4) The Minister shall issue a rulebook on the procedure for determining the fulfillment of the conditions referred to in paragraph 1 of this Article.

This is one of the examples with regard to the regulations stipulated by an entity level and what may be the obligations of the club to move forward. Sticking to the same law with regard to the entity of RS, Article 73[85] states the obligations of Associations (almost all clubs registered as such) are the following:

(1) The sports association is responsible for its obligations with all of its assets.

(2) The bodies of the sports association are obliged to manage the property of the sports association with the attention of a good businessman.

(3) For sports organizations that have more than 20 members, the supervisory board determines whether legal affairs were concluded in accordance with paragraph 2 of this article, that is, the assembly when adopting the annual report for sports organizations that do not have a supervisory board.

175. The club is obliged to be able to complete the necessary legal obligations of the relevant ordinary laws and that of the federations involved with the club. Clubs must also complete the necessary documentation and procedures with regard to the licensing of national and international licensing procedures to be able to compete in the respective league. The previous paragraph is mostly tailored to sports that have a regulation to the licensing aspect to be able to compete in a competition. The club's obligations are not any different to other sectors and have to comply with ordinary laws according to the jurisdiction of the location of the registration of the club.

V. Termination of Contract

176. To understand the scope of the termination of a contract, we must consider the perspective of unilateral and mutual termination by the parties involved. The National Football Federation has stipulated in the Rulebook on the Registration of Players and Clubs and Status and Transfers of Players (Rulebook FA) the particular ways that a club or a player may terminate a contract. Within the legal terms, the termination may be commenced mutually, where both parties agree to the termination or unilaterally, in which one party to the agreement has a right to terminate or

85. *Supra* on 31.

seeks to do so. The FA Rulebook, with regard to the termination of players' contracts, is identical to that of the FIFA RSTP regulations and therefore we can conclude that the national federation and FIFA have aligned such regulations. As stated in Article 80 of the Rulebook FA:[86]

> mutual terminated contract between the club and the player may be concluded during the season and the registration of the player may be completed within the registration period only.

177. As stipulated in the Rulebook of FA, termination has different components that must be considered and in line with the regulations. Considering Article 81 of the Rulebook BiH FA, the following is important to stipulate with regard to "termination of contract for justified reasons":

> (1) …
> (2) Justifiable reasons for termination of the contract by the club may be: refusal to train, refusal of rehabilitation, failure to respond to an invitation to play matches, as well as other injuries or work obligations that were often repeated even after warnings in written form.
> (3) Justifiable reasons for terminating the contract by the player may be: non-payment of salary, non-payment of other benefits, non-payment of pension and disability insurance contributions, etc. and violations of other contractual obligations.

178. Staying on the factor of justifiable reasons, another factor to be considered is that of justified sports-related termination. The above are just some of the main aspects of justified termination and would be seen as a reasonable means to terminate a contract. Under Article 85 of the Rulebook FA,[87] the Sports Justified Termination stipulates the following:

> (1) A professional player who played less than 10% of the official matches during the season performed by his club may prematurely terminate the contract on sports grounds and justified reasons …
> (2) The existence of a sportingly justified reason is determined on a case-by-case basis. In such, no sports sanctions are imposed, although the payment of compensation may be imposed, and the club has the right to request that the player return the contracted amounts he received in proportion to the time he terminated contract before expiration.
> (3) A professional player may terminate his contract for sporting reasons only within 15 (fifteen) days after the last official matches in the season in which conditions appeared for terminating the contract on this basis.

179. The above are justifiable ways to be able to terminate a contract or with regard to the mutual termination between the club and the player. In situations

86. *Ibid.*, on 50.
87. *Ibid.*

where the termination has occurred without the justifiable reasons stipulated and to the detriment of one of the parties, the particular matter may be lodged with the FA to resolve and receive potential monetary gain from the claim or can result in other disciplinary measures. The simpler way to conclude a termination, if possible, would be the mutual aspect, due to lack of any potential complications arising from such. Mainly, in BiH, the main claims submitted for termination are those with regard to lack of paying salaries on time; there are not too many with regard to playing or disciplinary reasons. When considering employment law on the entity level, the termination must be completed with a written notice, although both entities and the district have regulations set in detail, which employees may be terminated or vice versa.

180. If we consider the employment laws of the entities and district, the definition of the possibility of termination of contracts is usually stipulated within the rulebooks of the company or association and in line with the necessary laws that govern such. The termination may be completed in other ways with regard to lack of work for the particular role, but this is again not tailored to sports and the relationship between a club and an athlete.

181. When considering termination, clubs and athletes should be well informed about the ordinary laws, regulations and rulebooks, therefore avoiding unnecessary claims lodged against the other party. The simple way with regard to termination is to define the actual ways such may occur within the contract or rulebook. Once a player or employee has a contract that is terminated, he or she must apply for unemployment to be able to not lose the medical and unemployment contributions. Most athletes are not aware of such and therefore are left without medical care, unless they find a new club in a short time being.

§4. Agent Regulations

182. When it comes to regulations concerning the work of agents or intermediaries, this matter is not dealt with in detail in BiH, except for the Law on Obligations,[88] in which Article 813 regulates the "intermediaries" and the same provisions regulate the rights and obligations of the intermediary and the principal. The rules of sports federations are also essential for this issue, and this particular issue is changing with the current adoption of agents through the licensing process in FIFA. Currently, the only regulation in the FA available to access is the previous Rulebook on Intermediaries of the NS BIH[89] (Football Association of BiH), which regulated in detail the issue of sports intermediaries and their rights and obligations. It is important to note that as of 2023, the intermediary rulebook is no longer effective

88. "*Official Gazette of the SFRJ*," Nos. 29/1978, 39/1985, 45/1989—Decision of the USJ and 57/1989, "*Official Gazette of the RBiH*," Nos. 2/1992, 13/1993. I 13/1994 and *FBiH Official Gazette*, Nos. 29/2003 and 42/2011.
89. Pravilnik o posrednicima 2017 [Rulebook on Intermediaries of National football Association 2017], https://www.nfsbih.ba/nsbih_userfiles/file/Pravilnik.

and that the body of FIFA has revised the previous regulations. However, such has yet to be adapted to the regulations of the N/FSBiH.

I. Regulations

183. The only regulations concerning the specificity of agent work are the new regulations that FIFA introduced. Previous intermediaries will now be considered agents after they complete a FIFA Agent Exam[90] and pass such; they will have the proper license to work as an agent. Prior to being able to take the FIFA Exam, the candidate must apply to the FIFA Agent Platform. The FIFA Agent Regulations Article 4[91] allows us to understand the general provisions of becoming an Agent and being recognized by the international community. Article 4 states the following:

(1) A natural person may become a Football Agent by submitting a complete license application via the Platform.
(2) Complying with the eligibility requirements.
(3) Successfully passing the exam conducted by FIFA.
(4) Paying an annual fee to FIFA.
(5) By applying for a license, an applicant agrees to abide by these Regulations and the FIFA Statutes, FIFA Code of Ethics, FIFA Disciplinary Code, and RSTP, all of which are available on www.fifa.com.

184. The new FIFA Regulations are part of a mandatory procedure to be able to conduct business as an agent in the footballing industry. This was introduced since the previous regulations left room for lack of clarity and complications; simply put, the intermediary regulations needed to be regulated on a level to be successful. Therefore, the only complication that we have seen in the aspect of regulations on an international level is the fact that the contracts signed between an agent and coach/player can be brought to ordinary courts, and even if they do not comply with FIFA Regulations, the contract is upheld due to the laws of BiH.

185. The best step moving forward would be the implementation of the Football Federation on the national level and for the ordinary courts to respect that such regulations are in place to protect football. Unfortunately, too often, we have seen the collision of football-related regulations and those of local/national laws and how they differ.

186. After looking at football and through the research of other sports, there are no regulations or laws in the other sports that stipulate the work and regulate such agents. Therefore, we are left to rely on the regulations of the international body and abide by such; the only real complication is the implementation of such concerning national laws.

---

90. FIFA Agent Regulations 2023, https://digitalhub.fifa.com/m/1e7b741fa0fae779/original/FIFA-Football-Agent-Regulations.pdf.
91. *Ibid.*

II. Rights

187. The rights of an agent concerning the FIFA Regulations are limited to a two-year contract, while in BiH, such agreements can be executed over two years. There have been cases in which minors and their legal guardians have signed an agreement with a local agent for the duration of their professional career for up to five years. This particular agreement is void when we consider the regulations of the international body FIFA, but it is possible to be enforced within the courts of BiH. The only possibility to limit this aspect is if the agent would lose the license if such agreements show that they do not comply with the FIFA Regulations, but this is only to make sure that agents are then limited to taking the claim to ordinary courts, considering the threat of losing their license.

188. Another aspect of the new regulations adopted by FIFA that is important to notice is the fact that the agent can only be used once in a particular transaction. To explain, previously, agents worked as intermediaries and could represent both the player and possibly one of the clubs or at least receive fees on both parts. This is now limited to one participation during the sole transaction. If the agent represents the player, he may not be involved in the same transaction to represent the club.

III. Obligations

189. The fascinating factor that separates the current procedures of agents compared to intermediaries and previous FIFA Agents can be seen throughout the new regulations. The agent must now submit almost all of the work through the Agent Platform of FIFA. Some examples can be signed, terminated representation agreements, payments made, etc. It is believed that with this system in place and the Platform, there will be more regulated transactions without too much power handed to an agent in the transaction. The licensed agents must also comply with specific criteria to keep their license; one of those criteria is the payment of an annual membership to extend the license to the agent.

190. The National FA must implement the new Agent Regulations by September 2023. Interestingly, the FA can have harsh regulations compared to FIFA if it complies with the core articles needed to be implemented.

IV. Employment and Economic Dispute Settlement

191. Regarding previous dispute resolutions that involved intermediaries, as mentioned above, the intermediary, club, and player may take proceedings by submitting such a disciplinary claim to the first instance disciplinary commission of the NS/FS BiH.[92] Another process that the agents may have for relief are the ordinary

92. *Ibid.*, on 79.

courts (when the national level of both parties) and abiding by the contractual obligations, even though it would sometimes contradict the initial regulations within the National, Entity, or Canton Association.

192. Disputes have occurred in which ordinary courts of BiH have been used to settle certain complications. The intermediary, Petkovic, submitted a case against another intermediary and FK Sarajevo club. Petkovic was involved in selling Gojko Cimirot to Paok from FK Sarajevo. However, the player had a representation agreement with another agent who did not bring the transfer to the table but received a fee for the player transfer. Petkovic submitted such to the ordinary courts for a dispute regarding the rights of the player Cimirot. What is interesting was the percentage given to Petkovic for future sales (Sell-on for the agent) of the player; this agreement was signed a few months before the new regulations of FIFA were adopted and banned sell fees for third parties that are not part of the contract (Club and Player). He submitted the claim more than a year after he knew regulations came into place, the complication here is the fact that FIFA banned this kind of deal with TPO, but the ordinary courts were leaning toward Petkovic due to the dispute of the contract between the club and Petkovic for any future transfers from FK Sarajevo to a third club.

193. The new regulations have brought to light the possibility of complications concerning the FIFA Agent Regulations and national jurisdiction over agents. If we look at Article 3 of the FIFA Agent Regulations[93] regarding National Football Regulations, there is a clarification of particular cases at the national level. The previous Article 4, mentioned under item 2, states the following:

> The national football agent regulations govern the occupation of Football Agents within the territory under the jurisdiction of the relevant member associations and apply to all Representation Agreements that do not have an international dimension. Accordingly, the national football agent regulations must be consistent with these Regulations. In particular, they shall:
>
> (1) Incorporate articles 11 to 21 of these Regulations by reference.
> (2) Incorporate references to any mandatory element of national law.
> (3) Provide jurisdiction to a national-level body for the determination of any disputes, as established in these Regulations.
> (4) Provide jurisdiction to a national-level body to take disciplinary measures as established in these Regulations.

194. Article 4.2 of FIFA Agent Regulations allows unifying the system regarding matters that occur on domestic or national levels. However, remember that FIFA

93. *Ibid.*

is a body that decides on matters with the "*International Dimension*."[94] The international dimension aspect has to bear a situation that arises to a matter that is not of domestic level; for example, the transfer of a player involving a citizen of one country and the agent of another country can be viewed as an international dimension aspect.

195. It is essential to highlight that the same Article previously mentioned stipulates that the national associations must provide the jurisdiction of a national-level body to determine any dispute; this can highlight the importance of the collaboration between the national courts and those of the FA. Another aspect would be similar to those of intermediary, where claims can be brought to the disciplinary bodies that have the jurisdiction on behalf of the FA to decide upon the particular claim.

§5. Social Security

196. Social security is also available to athletes but only for those with an employment contract. If the athlete has a service contract, amateur contract,[95] or scholarship while a minor, these contracts do not support social security for the athlete. That being said, the athlete must have a professional contract or, in other words, an employment contract for which the employer pays contributions.

197. Social security comprises the following: social insurance, social assistance, family and child assistance, and veteran protection. In addition, the social insurance scheme includes pension and invalidity insurance, health insurance and health protection, and unemployment insurance. If the athlete is considered a foreigner in BiH, then they can also have social security, but only if the club pays social contributions every month for the athlete; in other words, the athlete has a professional or employment contract.

198. In a case where the player sued the club for not paying social contributions, even though the player had a part-time contract, the court ruled in favor of the player. Ajdin Maksumic was the player, and he sued FK Sarajevo for the contributions owed, although his contract was not an employment contract. The ruling of the Municipality court of Sarajevo was in favor of the player, stating that even though the player had a part-time contract, his involvement in the first team of FK Sarajevo and having a high salary showed that the club should have put Maksumic onto a professional or employment contract. FK Sarajevo had to pay contributions for all the years that the player was at FK Sarajevo, finally reiterating that sports organizations and other companies shall not avoid paying contributions just by

94. *International Dimension*: *See* decision 861307 of the FIFA DRC, para. 2 f.; *see also* CAS 2005/A/909-912, para. 6.4, and CAS 2014/A/3483, at para. 56, confirming FIFA's interpretation of the term "international."

95. In some countries, the amateur does not even have a contract, because this particular status means that the athlete is not paid for his work but rather could be considered on a basis of a scholarship contract or part-time contract. In BiH, all athletes either have a professional contract (employment contract) or amateur contract (service contract/part-time).

stipulating that the contract is not an employment contract. However, the obligations and rights shall determine whether the contract can be part-time.[96]

199. Unfortunately, there is no difference (as mentioned previously) between an employee working for any other industry and those participating in sports. Therefore, the contributions or social security are the same compared to other industries, which do not have special regulations for athletes. Contributions or social security is something that sports club must comply with as if it was part of the player's salary; if the sports club does not comply with such, it risks losing licenses, lawsuits, and having the authorities block the accounts of the sports club.

200. If a club fails to pay contributions for more than two consecutive months, the employee will lose the right to medical treatment in the hospital. All employees under a contract receive contributions and then have centralized healthcare allowing them to receive treatment at the hospital for almost no cost. Again, important to reiterate that the employer must comply with paying such every month for this to be active, and if they do, then employees retain the right to such.

96. Ajdin Maksumic-FK Sarajevo Opcinski Sud SA/centar (2018).

Part IV. Doping and Sport

§1. Introduction

201. In BiH, when we consider that there are vast amount of sports that participate in a professional matter, we must consider the background in doping. There have been cases of athletes being suspended from sports due to doping, but the amount of such has not been enormous; instead, there have been few cases.

202. Regarding doping regulations, the provision of Article 49 of the Law on Sport BiH[97] stipulates that athletes and all sports participants are prohibited from taking illicit stimulants, giving or encouraging their use, following the World Anti-Doping Agency (WADA)[98] rules. The Law on Sport in BiH establishes the Anti-doping Control Agency in BiH (ADA).[99] The same law defines its competencies within BiH and in collaboration with the codes of WADA. The internal use of ADA within sports organizations has shown improvement in the knowledge of athletes and sports clubs regarding substances and the use of medicine that can be considered part of doping.

§2. Ordinary Legislation Anti-doping (ADA)

203. The BIH ADA, in collaboration with the Law on Sport in BiH, has the following obligations as stated within the agency:

(1) Monitoring and coordinating activities to combat doping in sports.
(2) Proposing and implementing anti-doping measures in sports.
(3) Implementation of the conventions and codes of the WADA.
(4) Enforcement of the rules of the International Olympic Committee (IOC), the International Paralympic Committee, and the International Sports Federations.
(5) Managing the preparations and procedures for passing laws governing this area.

97. *Ibid.*, on 11.
98. World anti-doping Agency- governing the use of illegal substances as stipulated within the code, https://www.wada-ama.org/en.
99. Agency Against Anti-doping in BiH (ADA), https://www.ada.gov.ba/index.php/bs/o-nama/o-agenciji.

204. ADA has shown improvement by involving education throughout the sporting world in BiH from 2009 after the formation of the agency till this day. ADA incorporates educating the athletes and personnel and thus hopes to minimize the risk of using doping substances by the athletes. In 2011, the ADA received the "code compliance" status, which is for the compliance of the ADA with the WADA and the regulations set forth.

205. As found from the statistics from ADA, from 2010 to 2015, thirteen athletes tested positive for doping from BiH, and only three were denied testing for doping substances and therefore received a ban. It is interesting to see that the number mentioned above, more than ten, from individual sports, while when looking at team sports, we can see handball and basketball at the top of the table. Interestingly, the names found in regards to banned athletes due to doping, have only male athletes, and there were no female athletes on the list.

206. The process in which occurs the ban for an athlete in Bosnia can be seen as follows depending on the details of the doping matter. For example, a kickboxer, Slavoljub Budesa, part of the kickboxing club Panter from Bijeljina (RS), recently received a ban from the Kickboxing Association in BiH for two years for using a banned substance. Due to the illegal substance, the BiH ADA tested the kickboxer and submitted the results to the Kickboxing Association in BiH, which sanctioned the athlete.

207. Considering the above, with the involvement of the Law in Sport BiH and BiH ADA, it is essential to have further implementation by the sports federations/associations to have an impact on banning athletes from using illegal substances that WADA and BiH ADA regulate. The NS/FS BiH (Football BiH Association) implements a separate Rulebook that complies with the BiH ADA, and the Rulebook from the FA implements the sanctions for the athletes in connection to the testing completed by the BiH ADA. The Rules on Anti-doping NS/FS BiH (2017)[100] with the advisory from BiH ADA, as stated by Article 1.1, shall apply to the following within the scope of NS/FS BiH members and members thereof, players, clubs, sports technical staff, match officials, officials and other persons participating in NS / FS organization activities, matches, or competitions. The Disciplinary Committee shall have the competency to suspend the player and shall act in connection with BiH ADA after the results of such have been received. The suspension of such players shall be in connection with this Rulebook, the BiH ADA Code, and the WADA Code.

208. The burden of proof is on the BiH ADA to show that a rule has been violated and that the athlete has not complied with the anti-doping code. The Sports Federation does not prove that a substance has been used but can suspend the athlete for not complying with the anti-doping code and with the results received from

100. NS/FS BiH Anti-doping Rulebook 2017, https://www.nfsbih.ba/images/Pravilnik_o_anti-dopingu.pdf.

BiH ADA. This can also be seen by the NS/FS BiH Rulebook on Anti-doping in precise Article 15, which states that the burden of proof showing that an illegal substance was used shall be on BiH ADA.

209. In addition, for breach of an anti-doping rule that does not include a reduced sanction for specified substances, some or all of the sports financial support or other sporting benefits received by that player will be retained by the national sports federation/association and the members of the sports federation/association. The Rulebook of the National Sports Federations must comply with BiH ADA, the Law on Sport in BiH, and the standards of WADA.

Part V. Sport and Commerce

§1. Introduction

210. The commercial and marketing industry in BiH has much space for development. Sports organizations do not generate enough profit to consider such an impact, especially when discussing top sports like football. One of the key issues may be the taxation of sponsorship or lack of audience for the TV rights to be appealable to television houses. BiH is still developing in the matter of sports and commerce. For this, it is crucial to consider in the future for the Law on Sport in BiH to be developed accordingly, especially to a certain extent, underdeveloped matters.

211. In the MTEL Premier League[101] (First Division Football League in BiH), it is seen that the top four clubs have numerous sponsors, but in most instances, they are for compensation matters instead of money received by the club. One of the aspects that will be discussed is that all sponsors are taxed, while in some other countries, sponsors of sports are usually relieved from paying taxation.

212. In the world of sports, it has become known that marketing and sponsorship have had a tremendous impact on this industry. To remain competitive, sports organizations must constantly explore new technologies, laws, and relationships. Professional sports today would not be without marketing and sponsors (Bartoš, 2012). Therefore, it would be imperative for the future of the sports industry in BiH based on professional sports to adapt accordingly and be flexible for the sponsors involved in sports. To monetarize the impact of the sponsor, the critical aspect shall be seen in marketing and redefining the legal criteria of sponsors.

§2. Media and Television Rights

213. In BiH, there has been a significant decrease in total investment in advertising, and it has the same effect in sports advertising. When it comes to market value, the fact is that total investment in advertising has a downward trend, so according to the net ADEX estimates for 2017, it is BAM 70,000,000, unlike in 2008, which was estimated at BAM 110,000,000. During this time, there was a

101. Premier League of BiH received the name of MTEL due to the buying of the naming rights of the league by the tv house that is the main sponsor of the league.

simultaneous increase in the number of media outlets and a decline in the number of active advertisers.[102] The decrease in investment impacts BiH as a whole and the investment in media and television rights for sports organizations throughout BiH.

214. Considering that there has been a significant drop in investment, one of the key factors to start the resolution of the media impact in sports has to be adopting a unified national law for media and television rights. Currently, in BiH, no regulations or laws are adopted at a national level to regulate the media and TV rights involved. However, a few regulations are implemented through the entities, such as the Non-Advertising Law[103] and the Code of Conduct for Advertising and Sponsorship for Radio and Television.[104]

215. Considering the lack of defining media and television rights for sports clubs, it is difficult to gather the actual structure for sports organizations or clubs through the laws mentioned above. To understand the involvement of media and television rights in sports, consider the rulebooks or regulations from the sports federations/associations in BiH. There it may be clearer of the regulations on the matter, as the laws provided in general do not stipulate sporting events and therefore leave a gray area for understanding the structures.

216. The Rulebook on Media and Sponsorship rights relating to NS/FS BiH and Football Events (NS/FS BiH rulebook 2017)[105] stipulates the rights that the members of the federation/association have regarding media and sponsorship. Clubs that are affiliated with the NS/FS BiH must follow the structure of this rulebook, as there is currently a lack of clarification, as mentioned above. In the Rulebook on Media and Sponsorship Rights, Article 2 clearly states that the competition organizer may decide on the centralized placement of media and sponsorship rights. Centralized placement means that media rights for an individual competition can only be sold for a complete competition together and that individual clubs that participate in these competitions cannot sell media rights independently. Therefore, regarding the Premier League of BiH, it has renamed the competition to MTEL League of BiH since the telecommunication and TV company MTEL decided to be the general sponsor of the premier league. Therefore, it meant that a certain amount was decided between BH Telecom and NS/FS BiH for the sponsorship of the league and the TV Rights. The clubs were neither involved in the negotiation nor did they have insight into the final decided amount. The NS/FS BiH made available most matches of the premier league on pay-per-view TV, and the clubs were not involved in the choice of TV rights. Since the NS/FS BiH is the highest sports organization for football in BiH, they were able to agree on the sponsorship pack, and considering that all the

102. Arman Fazlic, *Neto Adex* and published by the, www.bhnovinari.ba.
103. Zakono Nedopuštenom Oglašavanju [Law on Forbidden Public Statements] “Official Gazette FBiH,” No. 101/2016.
104. Kodeks o oglašavanju I sponzorstvu za radio I televiziju [Codex od Communications and Sponsorship od Radio and TV] (2007).
105. Pravilnik o Medijskim I Sponzorskim Pravima u Vezi sa Nogometnim/Fudbalskom Događajima [Rulebook on Media and Sponsorship Rules to Football] (2017).

clubs are part of the organized league from the federation/association, they did not have to be involved in the negotiation or signing of the contract.

217. Most Premier League matches were on pay-per-view television, and the clubs were not involved in choosing the TV rights. Furthermore, since the NS/FS BiH is the highest sports organization for football in BiH, they were able to agree on the sponsorship pack, and considering that all the clubs are part of the organized league from the federation/association, they did not have to be involved in the negotiation or signing of the contract.

218. The naming of the league and television rights of those mentioned above sponsored had obligations that needed to be completed. According to the rulebook of NS/FS BiH, the clubs had to complete all obligations since they are a member of the Federation & Association. If the clubs could not oblige by the sponsor's contract, they would receive less remuneration at the end of the season for deducting points due to a lack of proof that the sponsor was advertised during the match. This particular protocol caused the clubs to believe that they were left out of the decision that impacted the amount of money they received for broadcasting an advertisement. The top four clubs of the league had almost all of the matches broadcasted during the season, but their main reward money for television rights was mainly based on the table's position. Therefore, it was a debate of whether it would be viable to move forward with the clubs that only the league position made a major consideration or whether another criterion should be considered, such as the number of matches broadcasted during the season for the respective clubs.

§3. SPONSORING

219. As mentioned previously, sponsorship in BiH is mainly based on compensation instead of cash sponsorship. Compensation on the basis that the sports organization advertises the sponsor for the compensation of the goods that the sponsor can offer; therefore, no funds were achieved by the club.

220. The Football Club FK Sarajevo, the club's general sponsor is Turkish Airlines, and the agreement is based on 50% of the cash and 50% on airplane tickets (compensation). Therefore, the club will advertise the sponsor Turkish Airlines through different channels and events. Such as banners, LED displays, on the official jersey, and using the logo on all official social media channels of the club (Facebook, Instagram, Website, Twitter, among others).[106]

221. The sponsorship that is applied to clubs has a basis for taxation. The taxation is classified as an indirect tax, around 17% of the amount given as a sponsorship. The Law on Indirect Taxation on National Level (BiH),[107] as stated in Article 1, is for the sole purpose that the term "indirect tax" shall refer to import and export

106. www.fksarajevo.ba, on the website the main logo that can be recognized is Turkish Airlines.
107. Law on Indirect taxation BiH "Official Gazette of Bosnia and Herzegovina" No. 44/03.

duties, excise taxes, value-added tax, and all other taxes levied on goods and services, including sales taxes and road tolls. Since sponsorship is taxed, there seems to be more contribution with compensation instead of tax. Therefore, the amount of sponsorship in sports still needs to be improved compared to the region and the European Union.

222. Sports organizations, especially those involved in Professional Sports that advertise a particular brand, must have a contract or agreement, whether it is on a cash or compensation basis. The authority and inspectors from indirect taxation of BiH may impose sanctions on sports organizations that advertise a specific brand but do not have a contract or agreement. There have been clubs that the authorities have sanctioned for yet to have an agreement with the brand advertised or where the contract was late in signing compared to the advertisement period.

223. Sponsorship development in sports: there must be a basis for the sponsors to receive some relief as they are advertising their brand and supporting the social importance of sports throughout the country. This must be considered moving forward, with a revision of the current Law on Sport, considering that only Article 68[108] states that those that invest in sports development and are recognized as expenses may receive tax relief. However, this definition needs to be more specific. Therefore, most professional sports organizations pay taxation as, in most instances, it is challenging to define sports development due to sponsorship involvement.

§4. Merchandising

224. The structure of the sports organization is associations, thus giving a setback for the ability to sell merchandise. As an association, it is considered that sports organizations cannot sell merchandise for profit, as the association does not have the legal framework to do so. In the past few years in the football industry, clubs were forming companies through the club association that is solely registered to sell merchandise of the club as well as import and export goods. The founding of the companies from the football clubs opened up the ability to gather profit from selling the clubs' merchandise. In particular, the associations at some point were not able to import goods, for example, sports equipment outside of BiH, due to a lack of regulation that allows for such. Due to this particular problem, the government of BiH made an exemption to the law to allow associations to import goods or merchandise. This is where we have a situation regarding the relief of the particular law but, in general, could be revised within the future, thus not restricting such, especially in sports.

108. *Ibid.*, on 11.

§5. Ownership of Sports Associations (Clubs)

225. The structure of the sports organizations is legally formed as associations, with assemblies, boards of directors, and administration composed. The fact that the sports organizations are formed as associations means that the club cannot be privately owned, and there are no ways to own stock of the club, as there are certain circumstances of ownership of sports clubs or stocks in other countries. Therefore, the Law on Association and Foundation only allows for the club's structure to be formed as mentioned, with the structure including members of the assembly, the board of directors, and the administration after that.

226. In 2013, the Football Club "FK Sarajevo" was the first club to include an investor within its structure. This was the groundbreaking first step to reform how clubs are to be run. Although the club can only be registered as an association, the legal framework allows the owner to buy the voting rights of the assembly. FK Sarajevo made the first emission for the public to be able to buy off voting rights and membership within the assembly, considering that at the time, the foreign investor gave the most amount of money and met the criteria of the emission, he received 91% of the total voting rights of the assembly. Although the club was not under the ownership of the foreign investor, he still could make critical decisions as he had the majority voting rights in the assembly.[109] Considering Article 16 of the Laws on Associations and Foundations,[110] the assembly members all have equal rights in deciding the association unless stipulated differently within the statutes of the association.

227. The Law on Associations and Foundations[111] Article 18 states that the rights of the assembly members are as follows:

(1) Adopting the statute, amending the statute, and other acts specified in the statute.
(2) Deciding on merger, division, and termination of work, the establishment of other legal entities, as well as other status changes of the association.
(3) The appointment and dismissal of members of the board of directors, if such an association exists.
(4) Adopting reports prepared by the board of directors, if such an association body exists; and e) deciding on any other matter, not within the competence of the other bodies of the association.

228. Considering the above article, the critical aspects of deciding within an association are reflected in the assembly members. Considering that FK Sarajevo allowed for the emission of buying the highest voting rights and as stipulated in

109. Assembly is the highest level of any association, therefore with a majority, a member can have the controling voting rights.
110. *Ibid.*, on 11, *see* Art. 31.
111. *Ibid.*, on 26.

internal statutes and documents, the assembly received a member with the majority of voting rights and, therefore, in certain circumstances, can be seen as an owner.

229. The reform of FK Sarajevo continued further; another football club was able to achieve a similar reform. In 2017/2018, the football club "NK Celik" had a similar effect; a foreign investor bought the majority voting rights in the assembly of the club and therefore had the right to make the critical decisions. Although the protection of the majority rights holder is not the same as if the foreign investor or owner of the voting rights had the fundamental right to privately own the club or have stock ownership. This is one step forward in investment in sports organizations on the national level.

230. Considering the above, the lack of definition and regulation within the Law on Sport in BiH regarding these matters leaves both the club and the investor vulnerable. It would be interesting to see what the impact would be in the sporting world if the sports organizations were allowed to have ownership of the organization.

§6. Gambling in Bosnia and Herzegovina

231. BiH has one of the highest amounts of betting companies in Europe. It is considered that every few kilometers, there is a betting company and not even consider the online betting platforms. Considering the enormous amount of betting companies throughout BiH and the fact that a high number of people are using betting companies, regulation needs to be set in place. The entities have adopted regulations on each territory, but there needs to be a unified national comprehensive law regulating betting companies. That law is considered ineffective because BiH has the highest number of betting shops per resident in Europe.

232. Law on Gambling and Prizes in FBiH[112] Article 2 states that for this Act, gambling is considered to be a game in which the payment of a certain amount allows participants to win money, property, or rights whereby the result of the game does not depend on the knowledge or skill of the participant of the game. However, the Law on Gambling and Prizes in RS is more detailed than the Federation, especially if we consider Article 5, which goes into precise detail about what is considered part of the jurisdiction of the particular law. To resolve the complications, the need for a unified national law would assist in setting particular standards and definitions for all entities.

233. The Republika Srpska (RS) entity has changed the laws regarding gambling and therefore has become stricter in making sure that this particular segment is well-regulated, while the Federation (FBiH) requires reform. The Law on Gambling in FBiH did not change much compared to adopting such a law approximately twenty years ago. A comparison can be seen in the details of the two entities

112. Zakon o Igrama na Sreču FBiH, Nos. 48/15 and 60/15, [Law on Gambling and Prizes FBiH].

(leaving out the current Brcko District). The Law on Gambling of the FBiH inherited the provisions of the previous law by which the proceeds of gambling, after deducting the deeds for the prize fund and the development of the Lottery, are paid directly into the budget without prescribing any criteria and ways of further distribution. However, in RS, the Law on Gambling stipulates that the funds will be used to finance humanitarian, disability, sports, and other programs and organizations. Although, in both cases, it has been shown that there has been a lack of transparency in the distribution of the funds after they are received.

234. Only recently has a change to the FBiH regulation, implementing more approaches to where the funds would be allocated. This shall be important to follow, not just to invite the reform of laws but to ensure that the practice follows the initiative. Previously, the FBiH law on gambling was proven to go against International standards because it neither prescribed the goal of gambling nor the primary purpose of the funds raised and, in particular, did not prescribe the criteria of that allocation but left it to the Governing Board of the Lottery of BiH, the Ministry of Finance and the Government of the FBiH the freedom to distribute funds as they see fit.[113]

235. The Brcko District gambling is regulated by the Law on Gambling and Fun Games,[114] and Article 3 of the Law states that games of opportunity are organized to secure means of satisfaction needed in the field of social-humanitarian activities, physical culture and sports programs and activities of youth, as well as for other purposes. Consequently, the regulation stipulates that the funds received shall be used for and allocated only to the above. However, funds from gambling in the Brcko District are based on taxes on gambling profits and taxes on the organization of games of opportunity and fees (concessions) for the organization of games of opportunity. The funds are paid into the district budget like any other taxes and then distributed to the beneficiaries according to individual decisions of the District Government.

236. One of the critical aspects of gambling and betting in BiH should be harmonizing the three entity laws (RS, FBiH, and Brcko District). However, in most essences, the current laws of the entities for betting and gambling differ. Therefore, no unified law on the National level will simplify the structure.

113. Centri Civilnih Iicijativa "*Gdje Ide Novac od Igara na Sreću? I Gdje bi Trebao Ići ?!" [Where does the Money from Gabling go toward and where should it go?] (2005).*

114. Zakon *o igrama na sreću I zabavnim igrama Brcko* [Laws on Gambling of Brcko] "Official Gazette" No. 37/04.

Part VI. Sport and Covid-19

Introduction

237. The COVID-19 disease hit the world community inexpediently in 2019, starting in China and quickly dispersing to the world. This disease was unknown to the world but quickly changed the lives of many, and just as many lost their lives from the disease. The SARS-CoV-2 virus causes this infectious disease and commonly infects people from contact with someone who already has the disease or from a contaminated substance. The community was trying hard to find ways to reduce the infection of people, but the disease was very new and therefore caused the shutdown throughout the world. Communities had to find ways to live with masks and a distance from other people, not to mention the distance from families and friends.

238. Each country took different measures to try and react to COVID-19, but in most instances, people could not live everyday life and mostly could not go to work (unless the person worked online). Some companies turned to an online video platform to assist in meetings and try to continue certain parts of work. Regarding live Sports, the world stopped, and competitions were impossible for training. The fact that people have contact during sports gave rise to the possibility of receiving the COVID-19 disease. The pandemic also caused people to stay within their homes and had specific quarantine measures or ones the government adopted.

§1. Governmental Measures

239. BiH reacted in the first instance by adopting a curfew from 18:00h till 06:00; no persons may be on the streets or driving around unless they have an exemption, such as hospital workers or police. Another measure taken was to have a curfew and quarantine for twenty-four hours for those under the age of 12 and those over the age of 65, considering the vulnerability of the two groups regarding receiving the virus or being able to fight it off due to old age.

240. BiH adopted a few decisions concerning the state of emergency due to COVID disease. One of the decisions on a national level was to adopt a state of emergency in BiH, which allowed it to define which government body shall take the necessary measures during the pandemic. As stated in the decision, the Council of Ministers shall form a committee to coordinate, regulate, and find resolutions within the country for the COVID-19 virus. Next to the mentioned committee, the Headquarters of Civil Protection of Entities and Brčko District of BiH shall commence measures to help take the necessary measures to stop the spread of the virus. Civil protection made the steps in the particular entity and district and implemented such throughout the Cantons and state level.

§2. Sports Associations (Federations, Leagues, Clubs)Measures

241. The civil protection committee, the national associations/federations, and the Olympic committee worked together to form the best steps for athletes and clubs during the COVID-19 pandemic. During the first three months between March to May 2020, clubs and athletes were not allowed to train, nor were there any competitions during this period. The clubs only started training in June 2020, and other athletes, with special provisions in place regarding training procedures, matches, and spectators. For example, Football Clubs had online meetings with the FA to implement the procedures to return to play. The FA gave initial guidelines but nicely asked the clubs to submit the procedure that the club will take to avoid spreading the virus. Examples of such were not showering at the training premises, arriving and leaving in masks, and taking a temperature before entering the training ground.

242. Within the National FA, under section 9, the particular chapter details the impact of COVID and the way that clubs and players should react with regard to contract stability. Clubs had to take a PCR test before the match was held, and the FA assisted in funding the tests to help ease the financial burden on the clubs. Any person that has tested positive automatically must enter a fourteen-day quarantine. This event was essential but impacted the sporting side, with some teams having difficulty competing with many players infected with the virus. Even though a team would have many members infected, the club may use the youth players but must try and complete the match.

243. During training and matches, only a limited number of persons were involved. Therefore, only some of the employees could be simultaneous during such. This was to limit the possibility of infection and allow only the needed athletes and persons to be involved during the matches and training.

244. Regarding attendance during matches, it is essential to mention that spectators were only allowed for part of the year in 2020 and the beginning of 2021. The maximum number, for example, in football matches was fifty per team, including players, staff, and administration during matches. The number gave limited ability during matches and also caused much with regard to the clubs' profits due to lack of audience.

245. After 2021, clubs were allowed to have spectators but for a limited number depending on the stands. The importance was that the stands had to have two empty seats in between and marked in a particular way with a "red x" for seats not to be used and a "green check mark" for the seats that were allowed for the seats. Also, there were disinfection stations at the stadium entrance with non-contact thermometers that would only allow those that do not have a temperature. This was an added complication due to the funds needed by the clubs to organize the personnel at the entrance and with the needed supplies to ensure that people followed the instructions. During matches, the spectators had to wear facemasks as well to avoid the possibility of any spread of the COVID-19 virus.

246. Football clubs and sports teams, when traveling, had to always travel with two buses. By airplane, it would need to be a charter airplane used with the idea of players and staff spreading apart while on the airplane. Another reason why Football Clubs and sports teams had financial complications was due to the lack of profit but the numerous needs for spending on the particular measures in place.

247. Eventually, when there was a vaccine for the COVID-19 Virus, live sports returned to the way it was prior to the global pandemic. Nevertheless, live sports have taken a hit regarding the loss of financial profit during COVID-19 and are still recovering from a financial standpoint. During COVID-19, sports were not able to generate the same profit as before, therefore, clubs started becoming creative in keeping their fans engaged, even if it is just online or creative ways for match days when fans were not allowed to attend.

§3. Concluding Remarks

248. BiH is a relativity young country, considering the moment it established independence from Yugoslavia. The ability to adopt laws and legislative systems within BiH has been a slow process; therefore, sports law regulations need more effective support. The current sports legislative system is a start, but it would be essential to change and develop it according to the needs of such. Currently, the major complication within BiH is the confusion of the jurisdiction and the lengthy trial period before the claim is resolved. Many other improvements may be considered, but solving the length and jurisdiction complications would be the effective change needed. Sports in BiH are developing, and for this to occur in the most effective way, the regulations and laws of sports should follow a similar path. The next steps of sports law are important to the development of the country and the way sports are regulated.

Selected Bibliography

Works Cited

(1995). *Daytona Framework Agreement.* n/a.

Governmental Structure of Bosnia and Herzegovina. (November 12, 2007). Retrieved from Public Intelligence: https://info.publicintelligence.net/CPS131107.pdf.

(2007). *A cobbled Together Justice System.* The Center for Investigative Reporting.

Law on Sport Bosnia and Herzegovina. (2017). *Zakon o Sportu BiH 90/17.* Bosnia and Herzegovina: Prnjavorac.

Zakon o Sportu RS, Sl. glasnik, br. 4/2002, 66/2003, 73/2008, 102/2008 (RS).

Zakon o Sprecivanju Nasilja na Sportskim Priredbima, 106/15 (Republika Srpska 2015).

Walrave & Koch v. Association Union Cycliste Internationale "Walrave," 36/74 (ECR 1405).

Zakon o Udruzenjima i Fondacijama BiH. (n.d.). Retrieved from MPR: http://www.mpr.gov.ba/biblioteka/zakoni/bs/Zakon%20o%20udruzenjima%20i%20fondacijama%20-%2032%20-%2001.pdf.

Zakon o Udruzenjima i Fondacijama Brcko District. (2002). Retrieved from Skupstinabd: https://skupstinabd.ba/3-zakon/hr/Zakon%20o%20udrugama%20i%20fondacijama/001%2012-02%20Zakon%20o%20udrugama%20i%20fundacijama.pdf.

Zakon o Strancima. (2015/2021). Retrieved from Zakon o Strancima: https://www.paragraf.ba/propisi/bih/zakon-o-strancima.html.

Zakon o Porezu Na Dohodak. (10/08, 9/10, 44/11, 7/13 i 65/13). Retrieved from UPFBIH: http://www.upfbih.ba/uimages/dokumenti/d9bf6-zakon-o-porezu-na-dohodak-ispravan-tekst.pdf.

Zakon o Doprinosima. (35/98). Retrieved from pufbih: https://www.pufbih.ba/v1/public/upload/zakoni/556b3-zakon_o_doprinosima_35_98-hr.pdf.

McCann, M. A. (2012). *Oxford Handbook of American Sports Law.* Oxford Books.

Prnjavorac. (2015). *Zakon o Prekršanjima BiH.* Retrieved from Prnjavorac: https://advokat-prnjavorac.com/zakoni/Zakon_o_prekrsajima.pdf.

Tort Law in Sports. (n.d.). *Jrank Law.*

Staff, R. (2008). *Croatian Player Dies after hitting head on wall.* Retrieved from Reuters: https://www.reuters.com/article/soccer-europe-croatia-death-idUKL0393548520080403.

Selected Bibliography

Loland, S. (2007). Justice in Sport: An Ideal and its interpretations. *Sports, Ethics, and Philosphy*, 78–95.

National Olympic Comittee of BiH. (n.d.). Retrieved from okbih: http://www.okbih.ba .

National Football Association of BiH. (n.d.). Retrieved from nfsbih: https://www.nfsbih.ba/.

Republika Srpska Football Association. (n.d.). Retrieved from fsrs: https://fsrs.org/sr-BA/.

The Football Associations of the Federations. (n.d.). Retrieved from nsfbih: http://www.nsfbih.ba.

Football Association of Federation. (n.d.). Retrieved from nfsbih: https://www.nsfbih.ba/.

Rulebook on the Registration of Players and Clubs and Status and Transfer of Players. (2021). Retrieved from https://www.nfsbih.ba/images/2021-D/Dokumenti_2021/Pravilnik_o_registracijama_klubova_i_igra%C4%8Da_i_statusu_i_transferu_igra%C4%8Da_2021_1._KONA%C4%8CNI_PRINT_WEB.pdf.

Hadzic, M. (2018). *Izvori Radnog Prava*. Sarajevo.

Employment Law in FBiH. (26/16). Federation, Bosnia and Herzegovina.

Consitution of BiH. (25/09). BiH.

National Football Association of BiH. (n.d.). Retrieved from nfsbih: https://www.nfsbih.ba/savez/propisi/.

Transparency International. (2007). Retrieved from ti-bih: https://ti-bih.org/?lang=en.

Ministry of Sport KS. (n.d.). Retrieved from mks: https://mks.ks.gov.ba/sektori/sport.

Ministry of Family, Youth, and Sport (RS). (n.d.). Retrieved from Vlada RS: https://www.vladars.net/sr-SP-Cyrl/Vlada/Ministarstva/mpos/oSport/Pages/Splash.aspx.

Law on Gender Equality in Bosnia and Herzegovina. (2010). Retrieved from osce: https://www.osce.org/files/f/documents/e/0/126173.pdf.

Laws on Association and Foundations. (94/16). Retrieved from Prnjavorac: https://advokat-prnjavorac.com/zakoni/Zakon-o-udruzenjima-i-fondacijama-BiH.pdf.

Law of Offense. (2020). Retrieved from Prnjavorac: https://advokat-prnjavorac.com/zakoni/Zakon_o_prekrsajima.pdf.

Ensar Jusufovic v. FK Sarajevo, 65/0-P-698180 18P, 2019 (Sarajevo 2019).

Sarajevo Fan Died of Gunshot Wound. (2009). Retrieved from Balkan Insight: https://balkaninsight.com/2009/10/05/sarajevo-fan-died-of-gunshot-wound/

("Official Gazzet of RS," Nos. 1/2016, 66/2018, 91/2021—Decision US i 119/2021). *Employment Law in RS*. Republika Srpska, BiH.

("Official Gazzet Brčko distrikta BiH," Nos. 34/2019, 2/2021, 6/2021 and 15/2022). *Employment Law of Brcko District*. Brcko District, BiH.

FIFA Regulations on the Status and Transfer of Players. (n.d.). Retrieved from FIFA: https://digitalhub.fifa.com/m/1b47c74a7d44a9b5/original/Regulations-on-the-Status-and-Transfer-of-Players-March-2022.pdf.

Rulebook on Licensing of Clubs Premer League. (n.d.). Retrieved from nfsbih: https://www.nfsbih.ba/images/2022-D/Licenciranje_23_24/Pravilnik_o_Licenciranju_PL_2022.pdf.

Kodeks o oglašavanju I sponzorstvu za radio I televiziju. (2007). *[Regulations of Communicatins and sponsorships of Radio and TV].*
Zakon o Igrama na Sreču FBiH. (48/15 i 60/15). *[Law on Gambling FBiH].*
Centri Civilnih Inicijativa "Gdje Ide Novac od Igara na Sreću? I Gdje bi Trebao Iči." (2005). *[Where does the Money from Gambling go toward and where should it go?].*
Zakon o igrama na sreću I zabavnim igrama Brcko. (37/04.). *[Laws on Gambling of Brcko].*
Zakon o igrama na sreću I zabavnim igrama Brcko. (37/04). *[Laws on Gambling Brcko].*

Selected Bibliography

Index

The numbers here refer to paragraph numbers.

Index

Made in United States
Orlando, FL
05 November 2026

90230601R00059